Love & Profanity is published in 2015
by Switch Press,
A Capstone Imprint
1710 Roe Crest Drive
North Mankato, Minnesota 56003
www.switchpress.com

Library of Congress Cataloging-in-
Publication Data is available on the
Library of Congress website.

ISBN: 978-1-63079-021-7 (hardcover)

Summary:

A collection of nonfiction narratives
about the experience of being a teenager.

Designer: Kay Fraser

Kyle Minor, "Suspended" from *Praying Drunk*.
Copyright © 2014 by Kyle Minor. Reprinted with
the permission of The Permissions Company,
Inc., on behalf of Sarabande Books.

Design elements and photography in cover
and interior by Shutterstock ©

Printed in China.
092014   008475RRDS15

LOVE & PROFANITY

A COLLECTION OF TRUE, TORTURED, WILD, HILARIOUS, CONCISE, AND INTENSE TALES OF TEENAGE LIFE

EDITED BY NICK HEALY, WITH KRISTEN MOHN,
NATE LeBOUTILLIER, AND LINDSY O'BRIEN

SWITCH
PRESS

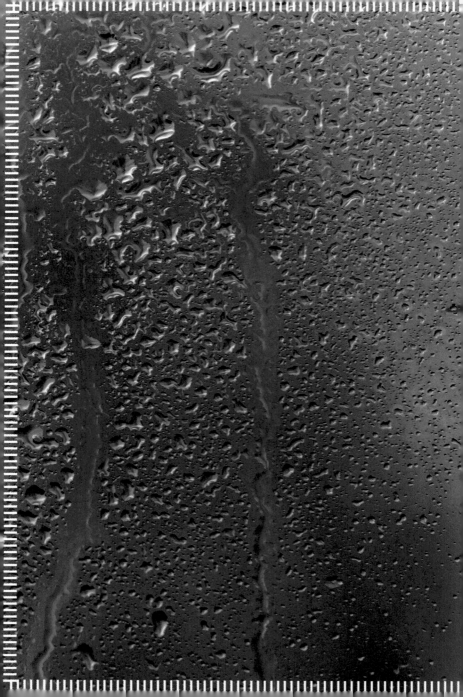

In his unforgettable story "Vietnam, Minnesota," Pete Hautman reconstructs an episode from his teenage years, an afternoon that concludes with sixteen-year-old Pete and two friends climbing into a muscle car driven by Mick, an older guy they've only just met, a soldier recently back from the war. On a highway leading out of the suburbs and into the countryside, Mick stomps on the gas pedal and keeps it floored. The car roars ahead. The speedometer's needle reaches 130 miles per hour, then creeps higher. "I looked at Mick," Hautman writes. "His head was back, his mouth open, his eyes nearly closed. The engine howled, the road ran wild beneath us, and I thought, 'I will write about this one day.'"

In that last sentence, Hautman runs head-on into the notion behind this collection of true stories. Experiences of intensity and surprise shape us. Even in the moment, we feel their significance, their staying power, and their potential to transform. That's true throughout life, but it's especially so during our teenage years. What we do then and what happens to us become the things we relive in memory and in stories we tell—to define and explain ourselves, even to understand ourselves. All of us, writers and non-writers alike, can identify with the sensation Hautman describes, a certainty that we are experiencing something that will become part of our life's narrative.

Gathered here with Hautman's story are forty-two more that present moments of similar impact in forty-two other lives. These stories capture the heat and intensity of teenage life, the humor and horror of it. Beyond that, they do what good stories must do. They entertain us and help us see our own lives anew.

—Nick Healy

TABLE OF CONTENTS

PART ONE: LOVE & PROFANITY

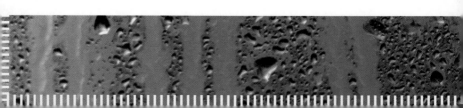

PART TWO: LOVE & PHYSICS

PART THREE: LOVE & MADNESS

PART FOUR: LOVE & APOLOGIES

THREE STORIES ABOUT WATER AND VOMITING

BY ADAM REX

I couldn't have been more than six and it was the Monsoon
Season: a month or so in late summer when Phoenix received
nearly all the rain it would get the whole year. That day it had
rained for three hours in a neighborhood with no storm drains,
and the streets ran like rivers.

"What are you doing?" my brother asked me. For a moment
I considered the question, sitting on the edge of the curb, my
pink hand submerged in the fast, filthy water, and wondered the
same thing. Certainly my mom would wonder later, when she
learned I'd spent the day with my hands and eventually feet in
floodwaters thick with garbage and pulverized worms.

"I'm fishing," I said finally. "I'm going to catch a fish." I then turned my attention back to the river, cupping my hand in the current.

"You're not going to catch anything," said my brother. He was three years older, and knew things. "Just 'cause the street looks like a river doesn't mean there's suddenly fish in it now."

I silently agreed that this was probably true, though the constant barrage of tiny objects (pebble, twig, something soft, pull-tab) against my hand in the cloudy water kept my hopes alive and then bump, my fingers closed suddenly around something big, the biggest thing yet, and I pulled it from the water.

It was a fish. A plastic fish—slimy, blue, a toy from something. I turned it over and over in my hand.

"I told you," I said, holding the fish up for inspection. "I said I would."

My brother leaned over and looked suddenly sick. His eyes were wide. His mouth opened and shut. I like to think he looked sick because I'd bested him, though it might have been just the garbage and pulverized worms. He was delicate like that.

"That's not a real fish," he said finally. "It's just a toy fish, not a real one. That's just a toy."

I thought this was a fantastically stingy thing to say. I knew it wasn't real. But I'd said I was fishing and not ten seconds later had a plastic fish and wasn't that amazing? Didn't that deserve something? My brother was petty, and I wanted to tell him so, but I didn't know that word yet. So I said:

"You're a turd-boy. You smell like turds."

Then I left, feeling just like God, and looked for a bowl of water to put my fish in.

***

When I was maybe eight or nine my family took a summer trip to California, and one of the highlights of this trip was supposed to be a whale-watching tour on a boat. If we were lucky we'd see a whale breach, or spray water out its blowhole, or do somersaults maybe. I wasn't really clear on what to expect. I think I was expecting a good time, though. I had the *Gilligan's Island* theme song stuck in my head as we boated away from the dock.

The weather started getting rough. Not like a storm or anything, but the ocean was choppy and the tiny ship was tossed. And quickly I noticed that for each lurch of the boat there was something like a little vinegar wave inside of me, breaking in the opposite direction. It roiled and tumbled, dredging up the contents of my stomach and squeezing them up into my throat. It occurred to me that I was shortly to have a blowhole of my own.

I blame my parents. Carsickness was like a hobby of mine. I once managed to get carsick on a horse. Really the only good reason to put me on a boat was if I'd recently swallowed something valuable and you wanted it back.

My dad recognized the look on my face and suggested I run to the rear railing. I threw up over the stern for something like an hour and a half. I didn't see any whales.

Later we made it back onto dry land, which I made some showy promise of never leaving again. My stomach settled, we went to dinner, and I had shrimp for the first time at an all-you-can-eat buffet. The shrimp were batter-dipped and fried, and I was at a point in my life when I would have eaten my own fingers if they were batter-dipped and fried. But there was something else going on at dinner that night—a personal grudge, a score I was settling between me and the sea—as I devoured a second plate, and a third.

* * *

High school is a flood, but I didn't think of her as some miracle I pulled from the water; she was just the next thing to fall into my grasp. A teenage boy *will* ask out a girl he doesn't particularly like, and I didn't particularly like or dislike Rebecca. I thought she was pretty, and I thought she'd say yes because I was a senior. So I was right about that.

We dated for weeks, maybe a couple months. And what a hassle those weeks must have been for her: Once I got a kiss, I tried to get a feel. After I finally got that feel, I thought I was owed it every time. She'd try to come up for air, and I'd only pull her back under again.

I'm forcing the metaphors now. Shall I say a high school boyfriend is like a shark? Because he has to keep moving forward or die? Always on to the next thing, never backing up—can sharks back up? I should Google it.

Here's the truth: Upon leaving a movie theater together (in which we saw *Mermaids*—this was 1990) we found that the far end of the parking lot was hosting a small carnival. Neither one of us had noticed it in the light of evening, but now at night it was impossible to miss. A kaleidoscope of light.

Rebecca wanted to go on a ride called the Whirlpool. A great metal octopus of a thing whirled you around while the love seat you were sitting in spun unpredictably on its hub. I said, "Let's do it." Teenage optimism is often indistinguishable from stupidity.

By the second turn I was closing my eyes, hoping that would make it better. By the third I was sucking back big bellyfuls of parking lot air and shouting for the carny to stop the ride. By the fifth turn it was too late.

It was hard to know where to aim; my vomit drew spirographic curves in the air. I managed not to get any on me. When the ride stopped, Rebecca found a single spatter on her lapel, like America's worst corsage.

She wasn't mad. But something tipped between us that night. She came alive—chatty, vivacious. I could have fallen in love with the girl that came out of the Whirlpool.

I was still woozy so I asked her to drive home. After a couple lights she grinned and said, "All this time I thought you were just a really careful driver. But you were mashing the pedal—this is as fast as your little car can *go*."

That would be a better last line if my car had been a boat. Pretend it's a boat.

Adam Rex lives in Tucson. He's the author and/or illustrator of a lot of things, including The True Meaning of Smekday, *which is being adapted by DreamWorks into the film* Home. *He didn't write his YA novel,* Fat Vampire, *to cash in on the vampire craze; and that's fine, because it didn't.*

BREATHLESS

BY HEATHER SELLERS

I was eleven almost twelve but I looked thirteen when I walked across Orlando toward my father's apartment on Orange Avenue. (I told him telepathically I was on my way. *I can't stand living with her anymore!*) I was thinking: French toast, snuggling with the funnies. I tried different ways of walking: fugitive style, fancy-bra-wearer walk, and a walk that always provoked my mother. *Why are you sticking out your bottom like that?* There were no sidewalks. Parking lots and sandy yards, sandspurs, sandspurs, sandspurs—on my tennies like jacks. I placed one sandspur on my tongue, green, tiny pricks, not yet ripened to a constellation of swords. To balance that sharp star in my mouth *and* walk well, I had to keep the pressure inside of my mouth even, and this super-hard task made me feel all the difficulty of my life was both manageable and behind me.

I held my tongue to the spur, and I walked and pretended. Pretended I was walking to church. I pretended I'd saved orphans. *Now aren't you sorry, Mother, aren't you ashamed?* I walked for miles. Men honked. I waved back politely, but what I meant was, *Rescue this girl!* I waved with both hands, quick. Honk honk, wave wave. I meant *Take me to your house and let's eat.* I did not know the significance of *she was found with no panties.* I didn't know what *no panties* implied other than forgetfulness, some kind of personal dirty. *Hey baby.* I waved *Thank you.* I was not used to feeling powerfully pretty, traffic-affecting pretty. At school, I was dark, mute, attractive as a hairball.

This was my second arrival at my father's apartment complex. First time on foot. Holley Apartments. Why an *e?* Why holes in the sign? Gunshot holes? There were bullet holes in my house. They're the opposite of eyes. I spat my spur, galloped up the outdoor cement stairs, ran down the corridor, dodging around the puddles on the lanai. At his door, I knocked and knocked and knocked. *It's your daughter!* I pressed my ear to the peeling blue door. Television, voices. The smell of cigarette smoke. Not that again.

That's when I remembered. In the woods behind my father's apartment complex, in the pine scrub, a girl's body was found. When? I didn't know time well. A girl from my school. Trisha. I loved that name, *Trisha*. Like tissue and winning, *tish* and *ta-da!* Trisha. Tisha? I loved her but I didn't know her. Everyone kind of knew her after she was found dead behind Holley Apartments. Her dress pulled up. No panties. What? This was 1976. Standing outside my father's apartment that Saturday afternoon in July, I saw a swath of my not-knowing disappear in a bright flash.

I watched myself from outside myself so as to not be so tiny and so hopeful, and when I turned the doorknob, I fell in. Couch, table, kitchen, all one room. It didn't take much time to see in the dark. I tiptoed through the smoke, opened the little half-fridge. Six pack of beer. Liquefying head of lettuce. I pressed my hand on the card table—stacks of mail, ashtrays overflowing, tumblers of liquid. Sticky. Slowly, I walked down the hall. *Was this my father's apartment?* The hall took longer than the entire walk across Orlando.

In the back room, an air conditioner up high in the window shuddering, banging. Blue-black light. My father, asleep on a bed that was half-folded, an L. My father, in the midst of being swallowed. I put my hand on his sock foot. I wagged the foot back and forth. *Hey there honey. So good to see you.* I watched the soft pink forms on the television screen. Surging synthesizer. *Uh uh.* Parts of people: a man's leg, a woman's breasts, a purse of skin. Soundtrack: urgent, dull, like pain. Was this like a murder everyone wanted to be in?

I survived, she says to herself sometimes. *Not all of you survived.*

Walking down Orange, pretending I was beautiful, pretending I was dead. Motorcycle guy, no helmet, at the light on Holden. *Wanna ride?* Close to home. Not that close to home. I hopped on the back and put my hands on the sides of him. He said, *Where to?* I did not know because I knew he knew, and the light turned green and I held on.

Heather Sellers is a professor of English. Her books include the memoir You Don't Look Like Anyone I Know, *the short story collection* Georgia Under Water, *a children's book* Spike and Cubby's Ice Cream Island Adventure, *three volumes of poetry, and three books on the craft of writing. She loves to ride her Bianchi bicycle, preferably in the rain. Heather was born and raised in Florida.*

GIRL FIGHT

BY JOEY FRANKLIN

Marty Manzoni's mother was fat. We all knew it, and we all knew better than to ever mention it, but that day in the school hall before basketball practice we were waiting for Coach to show up, and we got to talking about girls, as boys do, and someone mentioned Heather, a girl with sandy blond hair who carried her bulk around on ballerina tiptoes and told me just yesterday, above the noise of the bus, that she liked me—a girl with whom, against my better sixth-grade judgment, I had secretly agreed to "go out."

Marty Manzoni, whose mother we all knew was fat, had been bouncing a ball in the hallway when he turned to me, smiling.

"She's a fat girl," he said. "Why do you like a fat girl?" And the boys around us laughed because my secret had gotten out that day, as secrets do, and they had all been wondering the same thing.

I might have said that Heather and I rode the same bus for years, that we both liked football and sang along with Boyz II Men, that we shared the kind of easy, endless conversations that later in my life I would recognize as the first signs of a good, healthy crush. I could have said I liked the idea of a girl liking me, and I could have said that he was ruining it all with his questions.

Instead I chased him, as he must have known I would. I chased him down the hall and out the school's large double doors. I chased him for Heather and for my stupid, boyish pride. But mostly I chased him for the giggling boys around us who left me no other choice, for making clear what I'd already figured out, that I couldn't love a fat girl, that no one can love a fat girl.

Marty ran across the parking lot and onto the school's large green lawn, finally stopping beneath the flagpole, basketball tucked under his arm. I stayed at the curb and watched him standing there, his chest heaving, and then I opened my mouth and said the only thing a sixth-grade boy could say in a moment like that. And before the words—"Not as fat as your mom!"— left my mouth, I knew the insult would hang in the air, as insults do, and make the other boys gasp and shudder as it slowly settled into the ground around us.

Marty stood by the flagpole. Boys who'd spilled out of the

double doors to watch chuckled. I turned, still breathing hard myself, and rejoined my teammates as if nothing had happened at all, as if my girlfriend wasn't fat and I hadn't just breached some sacred boys' club boundary. But Marty inched forward to the edge of the asphalt and lifted the basketball. It hit me on the ear so hard I fell to the ground, my head ringing, and I cried louder than I have ever cried anywhere. It was an indignant, fearful cry, a where-is-my-mother cry, and the boys around me backed away, as if afraid they might catch something.

Then Coach pulled up in his car and stepped out, looked at me sprawled and bawling on the concrete, and then at Marty who walked past us both, picked up his basketball, and disappeared into the school. The other boys followed Marty in a mute procession past my body, and Coach held the door open to follow behind them. "Get up," he said in a voice that meant, "You're acting like a girl."

But I didn't get up. Instead, I lay on the ground, half hoping that Heather might drive up with her mom and see me on the ground and screech to a halt, jump out of the car and come kneel at my side and take my head in her arms; and the other half of me was hoping she would never come to school again, that I might die right there on the asphalt, and this story along with me.

Joey Franklin survived his fight with Marty Manzoni and is still friends with both Marty and Heather, though he's changed their names here just in case they remember the story differently. He teaches creative writing at Brigham Young University and is raising three boys that he hopes will be nicer sixth graders than he was. Joey's first collection of essays is My Wife Wants You to Know I'm Happily Married, *a 2015 release from the University of Nebraska Press.*

POWER DRIFT

BY JON SCIESZKA

I am eighteen years old. Rocketing down the gravel road in my faded green, only slightly rusted, 1968 Chevy Impala.

The '68 Chevy Impala is a thing of beauty—3,623 pounds of Detroit automotive engineering powered by a 307 V8 engine that can produce the 385 horsepower to get you from 0 to 60 miles per hour in 7 seconds. If you mash the gas pedal to the floor.

Which is exactly what I am doing.

By my own estimation, I am an amazing driver. I've driven these back roads millions of times. Okay, maybe thousands. Actually, probably only hundreds. But still—I know every twist, dip, and turn. I could drive them with one hand.

Which is also exactly what I am doing.

As an amazing teenage boy driver, I must always set a new world land speed record for any trip. Every trip. So while it might seem crazy to be driving 50 miles per hour on a gravel road that is going to turn a very sharp 90 degrees left in about 3 seconds ... I have a plan. And it goes like this:

There are two ways to take a sharp turn in a fast-moving car.

The first way is to brake gently before the turn. Slow the car. Turn the steering wheel gradually. Guide the car smoothly around the curve so the tires do not slip or slide on the surface of the road. Clear the corner, straighten front wheels, and resume safe speed.

The second way is to accelerate into the turn, yank the steering wheel hard left to swerve your back end right and send the whole car into a rear-wheel-spinning, dirt-and-gravel-spitting power slide drift. Clear the corner, straighten front wheels, punch gas, and blitz the straightaway.

Which is exactly what I intend to do.

But this time, as I clear the inside corner, I see something that isn't usually there.

A horse.

A horse in the road.

A suddenly bug-eyed and very freaked out horse right in the middle of the road with nearly 2 tons of 1968 Chevy Impala sliding over the gravel right at it.

When you are driving, you never want to hit anything. But if you are going to hit something, you are much better off hitting something small—like a cat or a dog or a squirrel. They bounce off—or disappear under your car.

A horse is a whole different, and much more dangerous, story.

An average horse weighs about 1200 lbs. That alone is bad enough to seriously mess up you and your car and the horse in a crash. But the other very bad thing about a horse/car wreck is that a horse is exactly tall enough to slide right on top of your front hood, through your windshield, and head-on into you in a very nasty explosion of broken glass and flying horse pieces.

That is one of the thoughts flashing through my mind when I see the horse.

The other thought is *AAAAAAHHHHHHHHHHHHHHH!!!!!!!!!*

I crank the steering wheel right, throw the car into a wider slide, blow just past the horse, and power drift completely off the road and into a field of dead brown cornstalks, still flying at top speed.

Engine roaring, wheels spinning, bumper snapping cornstalks plowing dirt cloud blowing ... I can't exactly remember if there are trees? a rock? a fence? ahead.

I turn the steering wheel slowly left so the car won't start fishtailing back and forth and flip over, and I keep blasting a Chevy Impala-sized tunnel through the cornfield, hoping to find the road again.

Down a ditch, up a bank, tires spinning, BLAM! I am suddenly back on the road.

I straighten the wheel. Ease off the gas. Position myself correctly and carefully in the right lane.

Stop sign. Brake. Full stop.

I look behind me.

Nothing but empty road. Well, also a huge new path of decapitated cornstalks through the field just past the 90-degree turn.

I'd like to say I take a deep breath, realize how close I have just come to being splattered out of existence by 1200 pounds of legless horse bombing through my windshield, and vow to never do something as crazy as drifting around a blind corner on a dirt road at top speed again.

But I don't.

I let out one long single-syllable curse word.

Then punch the gas pedal to the floor for 7 seconds.

Jon Scieszka: Born in Flint, Michigan. The second oldest, and nicest, of six boys. No girls. Author of The True Story of the Three Little Pigs!, The Stinky Cheese Man, Knucklehead, *and a mess of others. New series with Abrams about Frank Einstein, kid science genius. With robots. And a chimpanzee.*

POLYPROPYLENE

BY ALI CATT

Seventeen years after she's gone, you'll remember her lipstick:
a cartoonish smear of burgundy, cheap and trashy. The way it
flakes off her mouth like a disease, and the way she reapplies
it between third period math and fourth period gym class—
sans mirror, blurring the edges of lip and skin—salacious, as if
her preteen sex appeal is the key to running the mile in eight
minutes flat.

Maybe it is.

You run the same race: awkward and asthmatic, whimper-
wheezing all the way to the finish line at sixteen minutes and
counting. Gossipy girls sling insults just loud enough for you
to hear; squawky pubescent boys line up in the final stretch
to whistle and jeer you on: *Go, thunderthighs, go!* You yank at
the inseam of your suddenly too-short shorts between every

stride—yank-jog-yank-wheeze-yank. You long for the foresight to have worn sweatpants instead, or for scissors to carve the blubber off your twelve-year-old body. You wheeze and clock these miserable seventh-grade, sixteen-minute miles. Given the choice, you prefer research to running. You burrow deep into books because they are the safest place you know. You build mental dossiers on every strange thing that strikes your fancy: woodwind instruments, childhood diabetes, chlorine-based pesticides, plastic recycling codes, the Iberian lynx.

Here is something: The Iberian lynx is the most endangered cat species in the world. In the wild, young littermates often fight to the death, throwing each other under the bus of claw and fang—a survival impulse gone entirely wrong.

***

In Spanish class, the new girl claims the desk next to you. You stare at her—how could you not stare at her?—layers of caked-on Maybelline, acne pustules sprinkled from forehead to chest, oily black bird's nest of hair, homemade crop tops and stonewashed jeans pinned at the ankles, the lazy southern lilt of her voice. She is to small-town Wisconsin as kindness is to junior high: in a word, rare.

The boys call her "Scary Carrie" because nothing good rhymes with Carrie, and because to them, she must seem like a behemoth of womanhood—her twelve-year-old breasts already blooming out of a C cup. At lunch, you shovel starch and grease into your ever-widening belly. Across the table, Carrie fellates a soup spoon. *This is how Cliff likes it,* she tells you, speaking of her (presumable) boyfriend back home. She dips the spoon between her breasts and ignores, or doesn't notice, the spitwads flying at the back of her head from a neighboring table. You are glad that they aren't flying, for once, at your head.

The girls in your class call her a slut. Alone, quietly, you test-drive the word on your tongue. *Slut.*

It tastes, to you, something like self-preservation.

***

You believe in environmentalism the way some girls believe in white weddings. In your notebooks, instead of future husbands' names, you doodle triangle-shaped arrows with numbers and cryptic acronyms. They are resin identification codes for plastic, and you know every single one by heart.

As far as plastic's concerned, your town only recycles polyethylenes—code numbers 1, 2, and 4. At recess you lecture Carrie on the irresponsibility of pudding cups (poly*propyl*ene, number 5, nothing but landfill fodder). She eats pudding with her forefinger like a wild beast, scooping up globs of chocolate goo and slurping them down.

Later, you dawdle in a bathroom stall and overhear two girls at the sink: *I heard Carrie got a boob job,* they say. *I heard she did it with Mr. White and his wife walked in on them. I heard she's pregnant with her brother's baby. Gross,* they say. You slink out of your stall and approach them. These are the same girls who once tipped a beaker full of brine shrimp over your head in science class.

What a slut, you say. You cringe as the words tumble from your mouth. You half expect the girls to do something—splash dirty toilet water at you, barricade you in a stall and turn off the lights, call you a barnyard animal—pig, cow, dog, *something.* Instead they just barely glance at you.

Yeah, total slut, they say.

The girls leave you at the sink, scrubbing your hands raw and reeling. The inflicting end of cruelty is a foreign place to you. How shameful it feels, but how delicious, too—to sense your station rising one tiny notch, from scapegoat to invisible. You pledge to hold your own there, whatever brutality that might take.

* * *

Your speech on the effect of insecticides on the bald eagle population wins third place in a regional competition. *Third,* your father rages. *What shit is that?* Once, you come home from school to find him, paranoid and manic, on a mission to rid your home of flammables. The sheaves of paper that once littered your bedroom are stuffed in the kitchen trash—diaries, stories, a math textbook, all soaked through with bacon grease and wet trout guts. *Why you keep so much paper, estupida?* He corners you. *You want the house to burn down?*

You beg your mother for rides to the supermarket, and burrow through the grocer's dumpster to recycle every scrap of corrugated cardboard they've mistaken for waste. Even when you cut your fingers on sticky, dark things, you keep digging and sorting. You dig and you sort until your mother's had enough and drags you home.

***

On Carrie's thirteenth birthday, you listen to oversexed teenybopper pop in her bedroom and dig through her makeup case. You try on a vampiric shade of plum, wipe your mouth clean, settle instead for a neon fuchsia that makes you look bloated and radioactive. *Lipstick comes from fossil fuels,* you say, pursing your lips in the mirror. She rolls her eyes and tweaks the volume knob on her stereo until the bass assaults your eardrums. You try to dance. What it looks like is a self-conscious, arm-flailing, head-bobbing disaster. What it feels like, what everything has always felt like, is you and your body against the whole wide world.

This is how you do it, stupid, Carrie says. She gyrates her hips like a dreidel. You notice the glint of a silver bellybutton ring peeking out from under her shirt, how her long legs taper to such tiny ankles. You notice her pimply chipmunk cheeks, doggish underbite, the droop of her fat bottom lip. You notice everything, and it makes you dizzy.

Carrie's father, like yours, is a man of hard words and hands; unlike your father, he's a man of hard liquor, too—the heat of whisky on his breath as he stumbles into her room and backhands the stereo onto the floor. He descends on her, drags her into the hallway by her oil-slick hair, knocks her into the wall like she is a nail and he a hammer—a sickening rhythm, over and over until you think she might crack, sending bits of bone and skin and skull flying everywhere.

How ought you react to such violence? What protocol can a dizzy twelve-year-old follow but to keep absolutely silent, to crouch on the floor and cover your ears and bite your tongue until it's over, until she comes back in the room, face blotchy and wet, nose dripping red, the front of her shirt still crumpled as if held by an invisible clenched fist?

And when, years later, you begin to see how easily hate is internalized, how fathers break daughters and how girls break each other, how selfishness and survival masquerade as one and the same—knowing all this, will you forgive yourself for what happens next—the indelible moment when you see the bruises blossoming on Carrie's arms and think, *Well, dumb slut, you deserved that?*

* * *

You slip slowly from friendship to viciousness and let the fear of falling guide you. You sit with Carrie at lunch, but throw pickles at her back when she gets up to return her tray. You write malicious notes and stuff them into her locker vents. *Dear Scary Carrie, you are a nasty slut, stay away from me, I AM NOT YOUR FRIEND.* When the boys spit at her and pinch her ass in the hall, you do nothing. In swimming lessons, when someone unties her skimpy bikini top and yanks it off, you egg them on. What else is there to do? You are every bullied twelve-year-old girl who ever felt she had a shot at redemption.

* * *

Near the end of seventh grade Carrie leaves, as unexpectedly as she came—her locker cleaned out and a wounded emptiness in the places she'd inhabited. Nobody knows why, but everyone has a theory: knocked up, mostly, though some girls say she killed herself because she was so ugly. You have her phone number, her address, but you don't investigate. You swear to anyone who will listen that you're glad she's gone. You've won—survived—grappled your way above a sister outcast and eagerly dismantled her. But is this what winning ought to feel like? Vultures pounding wings against your chest?

Your knowledge of ecology is vast, but what you don't

understand is that a vacancy in an ecosystem yearns to be filled. That you once occupied that bottom rung. That of course you will again.

*   *   *

Field trip to a graveyard. The rest of your class makes headstone rubbings while you wander deep into the woods to collect beer and soda cans, all of them crumpled and sun-bleached to a dull silver. In the absence of a recycling bin, you appoint yourself temporary custodian of the abandoned aluminum, stuffing cans into every pocket and nook of your clothing. Maybe you do this because cans take two hundred years to decompose, or because they are as helpless as you are powerless; maybe you do this because in an odd-numbered class, you have no partner for grave rubbings—no paper, no crayons to scrub it with.

At the end of the day, you waddle onto the bus, cans in tow. Halfway home you feel the ants—dozens, or hundreds, scuttling up your calves, your forearms, the exposed skin of your neck. Down your shirt, your stomach, your back where you can't reach to swat them away. You wiggle in your seat while the boys around you chant. *Ants in her pants! Ants in her pants!* Something soggy hits the back of your head.

You make a decision: You unfurl all of the cans from your clothing and let them fall to the bus floor, where they clatter and slide to the back—destined again to be trash. You chew the inside of your cheek until it bleeds. But you don't scream, you don't cry—no, not until you are home and in the bath, hyperventilating and watching countless black ant bodies—tiny, disgusting, vulnerable lives—float to the water's surface.

Ali Catt grew up in Wisconsin. In high school she terrorized her mother, rode a skateboard, flunked creative writing, and got suspended for wearing a bra on the outside of her shirt. (Don't ask.) She now lives in Minneapolis with her adopted pit bull, Piggy.

WHY IS IT WET HERE?

BY CARRIE MESROBIAN

I will not get too specific. No addresses or real names. No times or dates.

The setting I will admit to: my parents' house. When they were not in it for the weekend.

This information was not like other information that passed around my high school, like tacos for lunch or having a sub in gym class. The information that someone's parents would be leaving their flag unguarded for a 36-hour period was not to be shrugged off.

All echelons of the high school caste system tuned in.

My friends, their boyfriends, their friends. My boyfriend, his friends. All sorts of peripheral acquaintances across the high school divide.

In this situation, all of us had to unify. Who would get the keg? Who had money? Did someone have a car to transport it? How much was the tap deposit? It takes a village to throw a proper high school keg party.

I was always very nervous about parties in those days, because back then, you never knew what would happen. It could be fun. It could be lame. It could get busted. Sometimes all three.

Of the actual party, I will give a few details:

There were lots of people.

Everyone, including myself, was very, very drunk.

Cigarettes were smoked.

Someone pelted peanut M&M's from the upstairs balcony into our sunken living room.

Someone who may have been my boyfriend stayed overnight.

And someone who may have been my boyfriend smoked too much pot and barfed peanut M&M's on the carpet.

There was one last key detail. This detail was that there was a boy who procured the beer. Let us call him "Randy" just for this story. And what "Randy" provided was not a keg. It was an object called a "party ball." A party ball was a new invention back then. It was a round plastic ball filled with 5.2 gallons of crappy yellow fizzy American beer. Probably Budweiser. This was a cheaper option than a keg or even a pony keg. And it was the best "Randy" could do. I wasn't going to argue with him. I just insisted that when he left my house, "Randy" take the party ball with him. Because I didn't have a car or a license and there was no way I could just drag that thing out the front door and throw it into our trash can.

"Randy" assured me that he would take care of the party ball. The next day, my friends and I worked like hell to combat the barf/smoke/beer smell with perfume and cleaning products.

By the time my parents came home, the house was too clean. It also smelled weird. Like chemicals and barf and the bottle of LouLou perfume that my father had bought for me from a duty-free shop on a business trip. There was an uneasy moment when my mother stepped in the wet spot where someone's boyfriend barfed and said, "Why is it wet here?" My parents were suspicious, yet I skated past any concrete accusation or punishment for several weeks. Except for the occasional random peanut M&M cropping up between the couch cushions of the living room, life was fairly normal.

Fast forward to my sister coming home from college for Christmas break.

"Let's play a board game," she said. We had lots of games in the cupboard in the family room. Scrabble, Monopoly, Pay Day, Trivial Pursuit, Uno.

My sister opened the cupboard and saw, along with the stacks of games, one cashed-out party ball.

My sister whispered, "What the fuck is that thing?"

I lost my mind. Because "that thing" had been sitting just feet from where my mother did her genealogy projects and stuff in the family room. It had been there for weeks. Because "Randy" was a shitty liar fucker. I could have KILLED him.

Sweating, my sister and I played the tensest game of Pay

Day ever. Because we couldn't do anything else. My parents were in the other room, dithering around in their parental way. We couldn't exactly tuck the dreggy party ball under our arms and go out in the December night whistling and saying, "We'll be back in a minute, don't mind us!"

We waited until they went to bed. I got a laundry basket and my sister got some blankets and a garbage bag. We swaddled the ball in the bag, then covered it with blankets in the basket. Then my sister shouted up to our parents about returning a movie to the store.

Then we wedged the party ball in its laundry basket manger all cozy in the back of my sister's pick-up truck and drove around, laughing like nervous idiots, looking for a store that had a Dumpster not in view of any employees.

My sister rolled up to Jeff's Superette, a little convenience store next to a hair salon/tanning booth place we frequented.

"Not here," I said. "All of my friends always go here."

"It's the only place that doesn't have lights behind the store, dummy."

"But…"

"Just go!" she yelled.

She pulled up to the Dumpster, which was around the back of the store. Casually, I checked the latch—it was unlocked. I flipped it open. It didn't even bang; a plastic lid! No one was coming; the night was dark, black, empty. Perfect. Why "Randy" couldn't have taken care of this himself, I didn't know. But I was in love with my own guile and craftiness as I reached back toward the blanketed ball and wrapped my arms around it. We were going to get away with it! I had a party, we had fun, nobody got hurt, it was all going to be fine. Any anxiety about it, any regrets or lessons or blowback were all quenched as I picked up that black-caped plastic ball and launched it into the Dumpster, the dregs of that perfect-crime party reaching for the stars.

Carrie Mesrobian is the author of Sex & Violence *and* Perfectly Good White Boy. *She and her older sister were raised in Mankato, Minnesota, by very nice people who didn't deserve such misbehavior from their children. To this day she is still known as "the bad daughter."*

M-E-L I-S-S-A

BY MELISSA BRANDT

My father left just before my second birthday. He didn't tell anyone he was leaving, but he left a note on the counter. I imagine myself listening to the tires of his car squeal as he sped off. He put me in my crib and left my three-year-old sister to toddle about until my mother came home from work several hours later. I know it was several hours later because he called my mother and told her he had left us home alone that morning. Mom rushed home in a panic.

When she arrived, my sister, Stacy, was sharing a banana with me through the bars of my crib. Years later, when my mother and I reminisced over the moment he left, our exchange was always the same: "I'm surprised Stacy managed to peel a banana at three," I would say. And my mother would laugh and say, "I'm surprised we had a banana in the house."

Mom had a handful of boyfriends and two more husbands between the time my father left and the next time I saw him, more than seven years later. He called and said he wanted to "spend the day" with me, then he took my sister and me to the Holiday Inn swimming pool where he threw pennies into the deep end for us to retrieve. The chlorine in the water burned my eyes as I struggled to dive with one hand and hold my nose with other. He let us keep the pennies, and he bought me a jewelry box, lotion, soap, a comb, and a necklace with my name spelled out in gold. M-E-L-I-S-S-A. He didn't buy Stacy a gift, because she had a different dad. Stacy's jealousy over the presents made me uneasy, because, even then, I recognized the injustice. She didn't know her dad either, after all.

A few days later, the necklace broke between the letter L and I.

Six years passed until the next and last time I saw my father. I was fifteen, he was forty-four, and it was his funeral. The news of my father's death arrived through a phone call to my grandmother. I stood in her living room and shrugged as Grandma patted my shoulder in an attempt to reassure. "No one knew his relationship with God," Grandma said. Her tight smile and lack of eye contact spoke to her doubt. Did she assume he was in hell?

His hands, folded over his waist in the casket, looked as if they belonged to an eighty year old. Mom said the frail, odd twist of his fingers occurred during the heart attack. It had been days before someone found him.

I sat between Rose, my father's first wife, and my mother, his third wife, at the service. Rose offered me Kleenex, which I handed, unneeded and unused, to my mother.

After the funeral Rose kept presenting me to strangers as Ron's daughter.

"Have you met, Melissa, Ron's daughter?" she asked the guests.

I wondered if my stepfather, Mike, had come to the funeral, and if she had gotten his name wrong. I'd only thought of myself as Mike's daughter.

Searching, I looked over my shoulder and asked, "Ron who?"

Melissa Brandt is an educator and a screenwriter with a script called Chicken Day *that is moving ever closer to being realized on the screen. She lives in Rochester, Minnesota, and loves to travel, read, and secretly record the conversations of her teenage daughter and son. She later uses these conversations in her stories. Seriously, she's not to be trusted.*

I DON'T BELIEVE YOU

BY CLINT EDWARDS

After my Dad went to jail, I started having anxiety-related
diarrhea. I was fourteen. Regularly being on the cusp of shitting
myself was embarrassing, so I lied about it. I lived with my
grandmother. She was in her mid-sixties and stood five-foot-
two with brown hair and a short round nose, traits she passed
down to my father and then to me. I suppose what I am most
ashamed of is that I lied to her. I spent hours in the restroom
crouching, grunting, and sweating. I turned on the tub to hide
the sound. When Grandma knocked and asked what I was
doing, I told her I was taking a bath.

"Why do you take so many baths?" she once asked.

"I don't know," I said. "I just like being clean."

She probably assumed I was masturbating.

Lying about my diarrhea lead to compulsive, outlandish
lies. I told her the school gave me a scholarship to attend Space

47

Camp when really I just wanted to spend the weekend with a friend. I wrecked my bike and came home with a black eye and scuffed knees. I told her a cougar attacked me next to the Provo River. I was full of shit, a truth confirmed regularly as I crouched over the toilet.

My lies came to a head during freshman P.E. The class was playing softball on a far-off stretch of grass. I caught a ball and it knocked something loose. My stomach turned, and instantly, I needed a restroom. I dropped the ball and ran, but I couldn't run the whole way, only in short bursts, slowing every dozen strides to flex my cheeks. I can only imagine what my classmates thought of me. One moment my hands were waving frantically, my legs in a dead sprint. The next I stopped and walked while clenching my butt.

There were two sets of restrooms. One was in the new wing. It was clean and had a lilac air freshener. The other was in the old wing, across from the metal and wood shops. It smelled of grease, wood shavings, and urine. Several of the toilet seats were missing. Naturally, the latter was closer.

Once in the building, I had to grab my butt and pinch it together. It worked. I was going to make it. Just before the restroom doors, my stomach calmed. I felt fine. I got greedy and headed for the cleaner restrooms.

Two steps later it happened. I lost it in my gym shorts—and found it in my socks.

I went back to the restroom and cleaned myself with toilet paper. The back of my shorts and the back of my socks were now a brownish black, but from the front, I looked normal.

I kept my back to the hallway wall and headed to the payphone, which was outside. Ahead was an open classroom door. If crossed, all the people in the room would've seen my shitty pants. I imagined it. One kid would notice first and scream, *Hey, that kid crapped his pants!* And then the laughter would come with damning statements mingled in: *He smells like a nursing home. He'll never get laid now,* and the worst coming from the attractive brunette in the front row. *And I used to like you.* I quickly crossed the hall. I was forced to do this half a dozen times before making it to the pay phone.

Once outside, I called Grandma. "I need you to pick me up." I said. "Right now."

She asked why, and I told her a nonsense story about a bomb at the high school. She paused, exhaled, and said, "Horseshit. Are you in trouble?"

I didn't respond.

"Damn it," she said. "You're just like your father. Whenever he gets in trouble he tells some jackass story and I come running. I'm through. Is that what you want? To get locked up like your father? Cuz that's where you're headed."

"I crapped my pants," I said with sincerity, honesty, and fear.

"I don't believe you," she said. "You're a grown boy."

We went back and forth, her attempting to uncover the truth, and me repeating it in a forceful whisper, hopeful that it would sink in.

Eventually I said, "Please, please, please come. And bring a towel." Perhaps it was the terror in my voice, or maybe it was that I asked for a towel, but she agreed.

I sat outside, my back against a brick wall, and waited. I smelled terrible. Time passed. I told a math instructor I was ill and waiting for a ride, I told the secretary that my house was on fire and I was waiting for a firefighter, and I told the truancy officer that my brother had an accident on a roller coaster. "A bolt came loose and busted him in the head," I said.

I don't think any of them believed me, but my answers were far-fetched enough that they didn't press the matter.

I was scanning the road when I saw Samantha Jones. I loved her. She enjoyed Metallica. Her glasses were thick with heavy brown frames that matched her hair. She was just the right mix of nerd and rebel. Sometimes she hugged me. At night, my imagination projected flickering films of Samantha onto the ceiling: Samantha gracefully ascending stairs and naked, always naked.

I tried not to make eye contact, but she ran to me, and like an idiot, I stood so she could hug me. A hug from Samantha Jones was everything. I wanted to get excited by her soft body. I wanted to smell her hair and her perfume. But all I could smell was my shit. We separated and exchanged a glance. She knew. Her nose scrunched and she swatted it.

"What smells?" she said.

"I don't smell anything."

She leaned in and took a sniff. I waved my hand in front of her nose.

"You smell terrible. Did you shit yourself?"

"No!"

I was a mix of anxiety, cold sweat, love, and lust. She smiled, grabbed my left shoulder, and attempted to turn me around.

"Let me see your butt."

She peeked over one shoulder and then the other as I moved my hips from side to side. She asked what was on my socks.

"If you didn't shit yourself then what smells like a turd?"

"I don't know," I said. "You?"

A pathetic childish refute. Samantha's narrowed eyes and rigid shoulders, the way her jaw moved from side to side seemed to say, *You did shit yourself.* And as she walked away, I knew she was going to tell everyone.

Grandma honked the horn. She leaned across the seat, opened the passenger door, and said, "Get in."

I placed the towel across the seat and sat down. As we drove, Grandma rolled down the windows and told me I smelled rotten.

"I'm sorry I didn't believe you," she said.

Then she told me of a time when Dad was fourteen. He called home and told her some cock and bull story that she couldn't recall. He said he needed a ride home. When she picked him up, he had a black eye.

"He'd been in a fight," she said, "and he didn't want anyone to know he'd lost. I didn't want anyone to know he'd been in a fight. So I took him home and put makeup on his eye. I did it each morning until it healed."

She didn't say anything for a while. Once our house was within view, she said, "I've been covering up his mistakes for some time. Trying to believe his lies. Maybe that's why he's locked up."

We parked and Grandma looked at me.

"People are smarter than you think," she said. "Telling lies will catch up with you."

She looked at my shorts.

"Go take a bath," Grandma said. "I'll wash your shorts."

Clint Edwards hasn't crapped his pants since freshman year, but tomorrow is another day. You can read more about Clint at No Idea What I'm Doing: A Daddy Blog. *It's been featured on* Good Morning America, *the* New York Times, *and the* Washington Post. *But that's not the real reason to read it. The real reason is that it will give you a glimpse into the steamy world of adult married life with children, and because he sometimes writes about farts.*

VIETNAM, MINNESOTA

BY PETE HAUTMAN

Me and Phil and Gabbs were hanging out at the Carriage House playing pinball and drinking Frescas. I had a pint of vodka in my jacket. Whenever Elliot wasn't looking from his perch behind the counter, I'd use it to fix up the Frescas. We were playing King of Diamonds, Phil bipping the machine mercilessly, slamming his palm noisily on the thick glass top when he lost a ball.

Gabbs slipped two matchbooks under the front legs, trying to get the ball to hang up on one of the triggers by elevating the front of the machine. If we could get the ball stuck on the trigger, it'd rack up points forever, giving us a huge supply of free games. We were smoking Old Golds.

Howie, Alpert, and some of the other older guys were playing nine-ball. Howie had this guy I'd never seen before betting five bucks a game. The trick with nine-ball, Howie once told me, is, "You gotta be violent and accurate all at once. It don't matter what balls you hit so much as you got to hit 'em really hard." Howie had played shortstop one season on a Twins' farm team before he blew out his knee, but that was ancient history. This was 1969. Men were walking on the moon.

Gabbs finally got the ball stuck and the points started racking up. Pop! Free game. Pop! Again. We racked up seven free games before Elliot left his perch and tilted our machine. He let us keep playing though, which put him in a good mood, for Elliot.

It took another half hour to play through the games we'd racked up, and we had to fix the machine again. Phil was lifting the front for Gabbs to slip another matchbook under the right leg when the soldier appeared. We stopped what we were doing to look.

He wasn't in uniform, of course. Nothing could have been so unimaginably uncool as to wear a military uniform in civilian territory. Still, we could tell he was a soldier: new bell-bottoms, creaky sandals, and a paisley headband that rested on his head like a crown. He did not need it to hold back his hair, which was medium short and combed straight down over his ears for maximum effect. His moustache was new too. He had done the best he could; the look was straight out of that *Life* magazine article on Woodstock. He carried himself straight and strong, but uncertain, like maybe this was not real, like maybe he was about to wake up.

Guys who had been cheating pinball machines and shooting pool two, three years ago were getting sent over to Southeast Asia. Every once in a while one of them would come back, buy a car, and go looking for their old friends. Most of them didn't stick around long—the old friends were dead, or gone, or just a drag to be around.

The soldier drifted through the bowling alley trying hard to look cool and aloof. He exchanged a few words with Howie and Alpert, watched them play nine-ball for a few minutes, then came over to the pinball machines and started plugging dimes into Eightball Deluxe. He bipped the machine too hard and too often, tilting it nearly every game. He said "fuck" a lot. He was drinking a Coke. I asked him if he wanted a shot of vodka in it. He looked at me like he was going to punch me, then said, "Fuck yeah!"

For all he knew, vodka and Coke was what everybody was drinking.

Gabbs and Phil went back to rigging our machine while I fixed the soldier's Coke. He asked me if I'd got my draft notice yet. I was only sixteen, but I didn't tell him that. I told him no, not yet. He told me it sucks, it really sucks. His name was Mick and he'd seen things I wouldn't fucking believe. He tilted the Eightball machine again. Fucking machine. I told him my name was Pete, and he gave this weird handshake I couldn't get right. Gabbs managed to get the ball caught. King of Diamonds started racking up free games.

Elliot was not in his good mood anymore; he yanked the plug and told Gabbs and Phil and me to beat it. Mick was suddenly my good buddy and explained as much to Elliot, who knew better than to disagree. These soldiers came back all wound up tight. Elliot said, "Okay, but these two guys," pointing at Gabbs and Phil, "they gotta go."

"Okay, okay," said Gabbs. He did not want to be on Elliot's shit list. "We were going anyway."

Mick said to me this place was a drag and was I interested in doing a little weed? I said, "Sure."

We followed Gabbs and Phil out into the parking lot. They looked at us, and Mick waved them to come on along. He led us to a brand new bright red hood scooped fat-tired GTO with a bag, a bong, and case of Colt .45 stubbies cold in the trunk.

An hour later, still sitting in his car in the parking lot, we had learned things about fragging, M16s, and Vietnamese weed. We learned how to operate Mick's bamboo bong, a technology that was new to us. Mick kept repeating that this weed was nothing compared with the good stuff, but it was the best he could lay his hands on the week he shipped out. He told us a story about being stationed in Da Nang and getting some little yellow tabs in the mail from a friend in California. Thinking they were speed, he shared them with three buddies before going out on patrol. Turned out it was LSD, he said, and it was fucking beautiful. Then Gabbs and Phil got the giggles over something, and Mick decided we should go for a spin to get our heads straight. He twisted the key. The engine thundered.

We headed west, four of us in the red muscle car drinking Colt .45 and talking whatever shit came in our heads. Mick had his seat tipped way back; he drove with the tips of his fingers resting atop the wheel. Phil wanted to know how fast the car would go. Mick pointed out that the speedometer went up to one-forty. Gabbs said that didn't mean shit. Mick said the engine wasn't broken in yet, but he figured, once it was, one-forty would be no problem. We were cruising west out Highway 12 at an easy eighty-five listening to Jefferson Airplane on the 8-track. Mick said we should all go to 'Nam on account of he could never do it justice.

"It changes you, the way you think," he told us. "Makes you know what's righteous and what's bullshit. You guys got to go there. You got to. Grow you up."

Traffic thinned to nothing; the Minnesota prairie stretched out before us. The new tires were humming, and we could hear the engine powering Grace Slick's souped up voice. We all stopped talking, for almost a minute. I was feeling a little sick.

Mick said, "Fuck it, ain't nothing' gonna happen anyways," and stomped down on the gas pedal. Even though we were doing eighty-five with a four passenger load, the car leapt forward as though from a dead stop. We were pressed back in our seats as the speedometer needle swept from left to right. I looked over at Mick, afraid to say anything. I heard Phil in the backseat: "All right! Fuckin' A!" Mick gripped the wheel; the needle passed one-twenty. The engine climbed a note. *One-thirty*. I leaned over and looked at the tachometer—not even close to redlined. *One thirty-two.* I looked at Mick. His head was back, his mouth open, his eyes nearly closed. The engine howled, the road ran wild beneath us, and I thought, "I will write about this one day."

Pete Hautman lives in Minnesota, where he writes whatever he feels like writing, from time travel adventures like The Obsidian Blade *to vampire-free romances such as* The Big Crunch. *His latest book is* Eden West, *a love story about a teen who grows up in an apocalyptic cult in Montana. His next book will include talking dogs, nanobots, and sasquatches.*

ISLAND GIRLS

BY KASANDRA DUTHIE

I grew up on two separate islands in Washington State, where barnacles and ferry rides and two-lane roads, canopied by evergreens, contained me. I believed a locket-style view of the ocean, framed by mountains and northwest clouds, meant safety. Now that I live in the Midwest, the water bodies are lakes surrounded by flat land. There are no tides. Where I come from, it's the opposite. The ocean surrounds the land, and the tides go in and out, cradling the girls who live there.

Age Twelve

Nicki and I find a bunch of dildos in her mom's bedroom drawer. We shake them while we laugh at the terror of us. As we're putting them back, we discover a cellophane pack of edible underwear. We eat the red sticky triangle until it slimes up our teeth. Just like fruit leather. After we wash our mouths out with sparkling cider, we ride the donkey that lives down the hill from Nicki's, with just a halter.

Once when we have eaten all the candy that we buy at Sprouse Rietz and we feel good and brave, my other friend, Heather, and I break into a preschool at the fairgrounds. Breaking and entering is easy. The door is open already, like all the others where we live. The space contains worn plastic trolleys and buses and Weeble-Wobble dolls piled in wooden bins. We don't touch them. We head straight to the tiny kitchen containing mainly a sink and a Formica table. On the table rests a yellow plastic ashtray full of cigarette butts. We can't find a light, so we pocket somebody else's butts to smoke later. A phone hangs on the wall, yellow too, with a dangly long twisty cord. We decide to prank call strangers in Texas.

We try some numbers we make up, but find no connection. Then we dial the seven numbers we can jumble, no prefixes necessary. We tell a whole bunch of people in our town, *You can suck it. Your fridge is running, and you better catch it.* We speak in Australian accents. After the hang-up and "WHO IS THIS?" grows old, we ride our banana-seat bikes around the baseball diamond.

Age Thirteen

Heather and I ride our horses, Thunder and Promise, at Jackson's beach. On San Juan Island, Jackson's is one of the only beaches where rocks don't harm our horses' hooves. We ride bareback, running through wet sand. The tide comes in like spider webs of shininess. There is nothing better than slick warm wind watering up my eyes while I grip Promise's mane. We ride until the sun goes down, and this is how life begins.

Age Fourteen

On San Juan Island during summer, tourists come, and there is work for kids like Heather and me. Two houses down from mine, a family owns a small business making greeting cards containing sweet sayings made from dried flowers. For summer jobs, Heather and I pick flowers before we dry them. Johnny Jump Ups, Lobelia, and others I don't know. We pick, and then we press them under thin paper sheaths and salty chemicals. Under a vice in the shed, we squash the flowers until moisture leaves the petals. We work with an adult woman. She never likes our reckless singing. She freaks out when the door locks accidentally. We sing, "My name is Luka, I live on the second floor!" over and over, all summer, and then I tell Heather my family is moving. I'm Anne of Green Gables, losing my most bosom chum.

High School

On Bainbridge Island, I find new friends, and mom calls us the "The Brown-Haired Girls." I lose my virginity to a football player one afternoon after watching *Saturday Night Live* taped on

VHS. I don't like this. I leave the boyfriend and go to theater practice where I dance the "Dancing Bunny Number" until the director suggests that I just watch the other girls while they run through the steps.

I flunk math and go to summer school with a girl who has a real-life stalker. I leave for weekends on road trips to go camping in Eastern Washington at the Gorge. I forget to tell my parents when I'll be back. I have another boyfriend who already knows he's a conservative. When we go to his brother's house in East Seattle, he brings a sawed-off shotgun. I break up with him when he goes to college. I'm sixteen.

The Brown-Haired Girls and I drive past parties at the beach near the military houses. Kids have named the beach "G-spot." We never stay or stop. We drive the Cutlass Cruiser station wagon to the ferry line, and then we ride to Seattle to go dancing at The Oz.

That night, outside in the parking lot, there are gunshots, and we laugh because we think the noise is fireworks. People tell us to run, and we do. We run back to the secrets high tides keep. We run back to the island.

I run back to the place in my mind all the time, where the bay tethers me to my teenage woes and the white driftwood becomes my pillow as I look out at the barges, large as cities. I sell Promise sometime around here, and I miss her. I miss my grimy thighs I get when I ride bareback in shorts with nothing more on my mind than the water, the wind, and running and running up and down Jackson's Beach, heading nowhere at a gallop.

Kasandra Duthie lives in Minneapolis, but she grew up on small islands in Washington state. She lives with her patient husband and two hysterical dogs.

PART TWO:

LOVE
PHYS

THE RANKS OF A MILLION GUYS

BY KWAME ALEXANDER

I'd tried basketball, but I couldn't shoot. I didn't want to get hit, so football was out. Naturally, my next step was to do what I thought any intelligent freshman in high school does when he wants to be popular, to be cool, to be noticed by Adele, the smartest and cutest girl in school. I tried out for the tennis team.

My dad was a tennis star in high school and college, but he didn't have the patience to teach a novice. So my mom bought rackets and balls, and even though she'd played maybe three times in her life, we learned together, serving and volleying weeknights and weekends.

Team tryouts were nerve wracking. It was 80 degrees but the competition made it feel like 100. The courts filled up with boys who'd been taking lessons since they could walk, and me, a confident, six-foot, pencil-thin kid with a tennis racket from K-Mart, three weeks of practice, and my eyes on the prize.

I made the team. Started at the bottom—twelfth place— each year climbing the ladder. To ninth, to fourth, and to first my senior year—crowned number one. All of a sudden, I was That Guy, the tennis star. Even my dad wanted to hit. In fact, on the first day back to school, the local newspaper ran a headline with my picture: "Can this Alexander be Great?"

My plans were coming together. Adele was a tennis player too—number one on the girls' tennis team. Three years had gone by with an occasional hello or smile between us but no real one-on-one conversation. Now, however, I had a reason to take things to the next level. We began hitting together after practice. She showed up at my matches as my personal cheerleader, which was surely evidence that we were well on our way to becoming bona fide high school sweethearts.

When I made it to the finals of the district tournament, she was right there. And even though I lost, it was the second coolest thing to happen senior year. The first went like this:

In the middle of the Civil War
right after Lee's Battle at Appomattox
and before Lincoln freed the slaves

Somewhere between stale
pizza and Robert Frost
and physics and the drama club meeting

I joined the ranks of a million guys
who've planned as much as an army general
rehearsed more than a Broadway play

Before asking you out
before being told
"I'll think about it"

That's right, I did it! I asked Adele to the prom. I approached her at her locker, just as nervous as I was on those first tennis tryouts freshman year. I mumbled and jumbled some words, before getting it out: "Adele, do you want to go to the prom with me?" In that moment, I felt like I was underwater and in an oven. At the same time.

When she answered, "I'll think about it," I was flustered and flummoxed. Two weeks later, near my locker, she came up to me and asked if I'd purchased a tux yet, to which I replied, "Why?"

"Pick me up at 5:30," she said, and right there, in the middle of Hall 3 in Great Bridge High School, I became the happiest, coolest, greatest Alexander ever!

Kwame Alexander is the award-winning author of eighteen books, including The Crossover *and* He Said She Said. *When he's not running two literacy organizations, Book-in-a-Day, and LEAP for Ghana, he sits in his study writing love poems for his wife and daughters.*

CONFESSION

BY ANIKA FAJARDO

The thing about middle school that adults don't ever seem to remember is that it can kill you. A new hairdo, jeans rolled the wrong way, a noisy bodily function in the middle of math class. You may not survive these things. For me, it was my infatuation with a boy we'll call The Jock.

His code name was The Jock because he was good at sports but otherwise pretty uncoordinated, and I think it was that juxtaposition that I found irresistible. He had blond hair and blue eyes and a sort of dazed expression. I filled the pages of my diary with tales of the Jock—what he said to me in third-hour English, what I said to him, whether he laughed or not. (Once he tickled me from across the aisle!!!) But for all the pages devoted to The Jock, no one else knew about my fascination. I was certain I would die if anyone did.

Then, during a slumber party, my best friend Alicia and I were in our sleeping bags on the floor of my bedroom. It was late, the lights were out, and we were whispering in the dark.

"Just tell me who you like," she said.

I didn't think I could. The thought of saying his name out loud—even in the dark, even to my best friend—made me feel like I was standing in my underwear in homeroom. I took a deep breath—"Promise not to tell anyone?"

"I promise. Tell me who it is."

My knees were Jell-O inside my sleeping bag. My palms were sticky. I couldn't see Alicia's face, but I could feel her waiting for an answer. My heart made that pump-bump pump-bump sound that makes you feel like the thing is going to burst out of your chest.

In the tiniest voice, I said his name.

At once, my heart rate slowed and I took a deep, shuddering breath. The feeling came back into my arms and legs.

"That is so cool!" Alicia squealed. She confessed to liking the Jock's best friend and immediately the two of us began planning a long and happy future.

Maybe tonight, I realized, was not the night I would die.

That didn't happen until later. At the school dance.

Anika Fajardo was born in Colombia and raised in Minnesota, and her writing about that experience has appeared in various publications. She changed schools in seventh grade but survived.

FIRST GEAR

BY MELODY HEIDE

I'm seventeen, and I sort of like this guy who sort of likes me.
At night we drive around our hometown in the coal-mining
region of Northeast Pennsylvania, a speck on the map. Blink
and you'll miss it, that's what we joke while we're cruising
down Highway 80. We're working hard on wasting time, so we
talk about the someday that's far in the future to forget about
the pain of the right now. His girlfriend has cheated on him. My
mother has just died.

Each night I sit in the passenger seat and he leans over the
steering wheel, his tall, thin frame folded like an accordion,
left hand on the wheel, fingers pinching a cigarette, right hand
clutching the stick shift. I see stars and dark shadows of the
mountains outside my window. We speak in lists: coffee, diner,
writing, art, tattoos, broken hearts, scarred mountains stripped
of their coal. He drives an old beat-up black Mazda hatchback

with cloth seats that smell of cigarette smoke and fast food and want and need and desire. The backseat is folded down and the floors are covered with CDs—Jimmy Eat World and Sunny Day Real Estate and Misfits and Kiss and The Promise Ring. Ska is dead, but emo is just coming alive.

One day my father takes me out to the mall's parking lot. He's teaching me to drive stick shift, and he tells me that getting into first gear is the hardest. It's about learning the skill of doing two things at once, he says. It's learning the skill of knowing when it's time to shift up.

I have my driver's license, my own car—a Buick station wagon complete with the way-backseats, the seats behind the backseat, the seats that face backward toward a road left behind, a road unraveling like an ancient map, a familiar landscape no longer recognizable. But it's an automatic and I want to learn to drive stick shift because there's more control, more speed, more freedom. Already I'm aching to leave the Appalachians behind. My mother has just died. I don't know who I am without her.

Push the clutch in with your left foot, he says. Slide the stick shift into first. Ease, ease, EASE but I kill the car over and over until my father says it's time to go home.

Almost every night I sneak out to meet the guy I sort of like who sort of likes me. My dad sleeps on the living room floor in front of the TV. My mother has just died. Dad can't sleep in the bed they shared. In the living room, the TV casts an eerie glow and creates an inky darkness. I tiptoe past him, hold my breath. He might know or he might not know that I leave, but he doesn't stop me—what they don't tell you about grief is how exhausting it is.

I meet the guy I sort of like at the 24-hour diner on top of the mountain. We smoke cigarettes, I write in a journal, he sketches skulls and flirts with the waitresses. In the car he says that he can drive stick shift, change a CD, smoke a cigarette, and talk on the cell phone all at the same time. We've driven down into the valley, and he's telling me it's a balancing act, a learning of how to do many things at once. He tells me that the point of driving stick shift is to get from point A to point B as fast as possible. He puts me in the driver's seat and I shift successfully from first to second all the way up to fifth without killing the car and we're traveling up the mountainside and he tells me to go, go, go like you'll never look back, like the cops are on your tail, like you've just learned to fly.

Melody Heide grew up moving between New York, New Jersey, and Pennsylvania but now calls Minnesota home. She writes a lot about the transient life, and her work has appeared in numerous publications.

JUST BACK FROM THE DENTIST

BY KYRA ANDERSON

The first time I had sex, my mouth was numb, just back from the dentist where Dr. Stanley Summer had peered down at me through his double set of lenses. Six Eyes, we called him, though never to his face. Lord knows what his receptionist called him—something scandalous, perhaps with a blast of air from the compressor, floop, up her stiff white skirt. I didn't know it then, but it turns out they were having a wild affair the entire time I was in high school.

It was a Saturday morning. My boyfriend, Ralph, had spent the night. His family lived a half hour away, so every once in awhile he was given permission to stay at my house. His parents assumed my parents would keep an eye on us.

Fools.

He stayed on the third floor, down the hall from me in my sister's room; she was away at college. It was a farce, really, a not very disguised one. I don't know what my dad thought, immobile in front of the TV—he may not have even known Ralph was there. But my mom practically tucked us in the night before.

She knew I was a virgin. We had been discussing that and birth control for months. Ralph and I had done every last thing under the sun except it. Sex. We'd kissed and kissed until our faces were beets, my hair a nest of frizzy knots. We'd dry humped every mound dry-humpable, explored every last fold of skin with fingers and lips and tongues. One night Ralph peered up between my legs with my father's flashlight. What's it like in there? I had asked, as if he was peering into a cave, doing reconnaissance for an overnight trip. It's very pink, he had said, ribbed, like the roof of your mouth.

I bounded up the stairs that morning, my purse stuffed with Planned Parenthood party favors: diaphragm, spermicidal jelly and applicator in a white plastic case. Ralph was still asleep. I climbed in next to him and in an instant we were pulled toward each other, magnetized. I remember that feeling now: eggs cracking open, warmth radiating, leaking everywhere. We knew each other's bodies so well. I want to say we were hungry, but it sounds like something from a movie, and yet it was true. We were hungry and without any shame or confusion about what to do though the mechanics of the diaphragm insertion were a puzzle.

I knew how to squirt the jelly in. See? I said, squeezing an extra line around the rim. It's like baking, filling a puff pastry with goo. I folded it in half like a turnover. It was sort of spring-loaded and, well, very wet, so when I squatted down, it shot across the room into my sister's hanging British flag.

I scampered out the door to the bathroom, holding the diaphragm like a mouse, tip-toeing naked over the creaking floorboards. As I rinsed it under a stream of sudsy water, my mother yelled up, Breakfast!

We'll eat later, I called back, noticing white stuff below my lip.

WHAT?

We're not hungry, mom! I said, louder.

Okay! she sing-songed.

I cleaned my chin—it felt rubbery and dead, slightly tingly. I dried the diaphragm on the towel and pushed it in before it snapped open. I had no idea if it was in correctly. I remember the nurse stressed that the front end—or was it the back end?—ought to hook over the lip of my cervix and I reached in to check but my arm didn't seem long enough.

Can you feel if it's in right? If it's hooked over the edge of my cervix?

Hooked?

Yeah, like around something slightly hard?

I'll try, said Ralph, my Ralph, ever game. And so he went back in the cave. I was on my back and he was kneeling between my legs, reaching blindly inside. His face was turned up and away as if he was listening for a distant sound to signal success.

I think I feel it.

You do?

I think.

Okay. I said.

I couldn't really feel his mouth as we kissed, wasn't sure I was using the right amount of pressure. But still, we kissed and rolled around like seals in a sea of sheets and comforters, pillows falling to either side of us on the floor. The wooden bed frame didn't squeak; we knew this, but still, we froze every so often as if the timing had been choreographed, listening for footsteps on the stairs, my name being called, but all we heard was our own breath, staccato on the inhale.

Am I drooling? I asked about ten times, patting at my lips. I don't think so, he answered, sounding out of breath.

And then we found ourselves back in that starting position, me on my back, Ralph looking down at me, his blond hair falling in a stringy curtain. His legs were between mine, his arms held his torso up and I slipped my hands between us, on his belly, palms under his hips.

Okay, I said, looking into his eyes, and he began. Stop, I said, my fingertips pressing his skin for a breath or two. Then, Okay, and he started again and that's how we did it, inch by inch, my fingertips tap-tap-tapping him in.

We had to go downstairs at some point, afterward. There was no other way out of the house. When we did, my mother caught me with her eyes. And it was then that I first felt her stare piercing through me and Ralph, and I realized that it hadn't mattered how quiet we had been, how many floors had separated us. My mother's fingertips had found their way to our sweet and salty skin, hungry for something that ought to have been mine, all mine.

Kyra Anderson lives in Western Massachusetts with her husband, writer / illustrator David Milgrim, and their thirteen-year-old son, an aspiring indie game designer.

AMBUSHED

BY ANDREW GOTTLIEB

A summer job on the paint crew at a local high school, the high
school I attended during the school year, and I spent long, hot
days in dorm rooms and classrooms redoing the walls for the
coming year. Cutting in and rolling. Easy, mindless work.

My boss was Richard, a tall, burly, big-armed man with
shaggy black hair over an ursine face covered in a thick black
beard. He was both jocose and distant, one minute telling you
something fondly, like a big brother, the next insulting you,
looking away like the world had let him down, pushing you
from him. He smoked cigarettes one after another, lighting
them, then taking them roughly from his mouth, blowing out
the first smoke in quick disdain as if someone had just told him
something absurdly stupid.

Rich was on your side, but he'd needle you every chance
he got.

Is this your danish? he'd ask at lunch, indicating the cherry pastry. When you nodded, he'd put his thumb in the middle of it and squash a big section. It looks good, he'd nod, chuckling. Enjoy it.

I was fifteen, and my painting partner was Dory, a brown-haired beauty with a smooth oval face, big breasts, brown eyes, and a slim body. A couple years older. She had an Italian last name. Her beauty was of a wholesome, approachable, and American kind. She had a boyfriend named Dave. She wore a distracting work T-shirt with a handprint of paint on her chest. Dave did that to my boob when we were painting the house, she told us. The cheek of him. I smacked him for that. She was shy and bold all at once—shy enough to be embarrassed but bold enough to wear the shirt.

Richard told us how to work. He had skills we didn't. Run your bristles around the rim of the can, lifting the paint out of the lid well and back into the can. Don't waste it. Masking is a waste of time. Go slow, one smooth line of paint. A drop of black in white paint makes it whiter. Prevents it from yellowing on the walls. Pure white paint will yellow. Paint dries darker than when it's wet. Use a fan for quicker drying. Hold your brush like this, up at the bristles, like you're holding a book, not by the handle like you're holding a broomstick. Is that what you call done? See that drip? Look from here. See that sag? Roll back over your work to diminish edges. Whaddya want, to get me fired? Do it again, the right away. This is all you've done all day? It's like working with mental midgets. This is what I have to work with. You listen to anything I say?

He'd roll his eyes and shake his head, blowing a stream of smoke, his hair sweaty at his forehead. He was frustrated with our youth, but Dory and I knew he was grinning, and we craved his insults and attention.

The rooms were always hot. The sun beat down; there was no air-conditioning. We opened the windows, and the campus was empty, so all we heard were the chirps and whirs of birds outside and the rush and hum of traffic on nearby streets. We had a radio that played classic rock. I could think about Dory's T-shirt all day long. We shifted our tarps and drops to where we needed them. I was jealous of Dave. I would cut-in the walls and Dory would roll. Or we'd switch. Once she told me Dave had to pee so bad that when he finally went he filled up a coffee can.

Take a break, Richard would say, bustling into the room we were on. Take a break. That meant we could lay down the brushes and sit around while he smoked, talking about things of a raunchy nature. Richard's girlfriend Michelle would sneak over from the cleaning crew and smoke with Richard, telling us jokes. She was slim with curly brown hair, a narrow face, and a deep smoker's voice rasped with cynicism.

I shaved in one of the bathrooms once. Dory stood and watched me. Can I do it, she asked? I let her use the razor on my face.

In the science labs, Richard would pick up stuffed birds and give them fake, high-pitched voices. Andy loves Dory. Cock-a-doodle-doo. Get back to work Andy. What the hell do they do with these anyway? He'd hold up a test tube, a Bunsen burner. Look at this glassware. Imagine what you could do with that.

I got really good. I could one-coat a small room in an hour and a half, trim and all. Later in life, I'd paint interiors for good money, always advising people to let me strip the wallpaper and replace it with paint, because I knew how to paint and not how to put up wallpaper.

I bragged about the bands I knew. Zeppelin, Hendrix.

That's what you call Rock? Richard spat. Humble Pie. Now that's a band. I saw Janis Joplin live once.

Dory and I were doing the hall at the top of a stairway in a dorm. I was telling her a story, a story I had that was my story of life and its value. I told it to people to seem wise. The story was about someone I knew who'd worked as a prison guard in a tower. A riot had broken out, and he aimed his rifle down at the yard. Then he quit. I couldn't do it, he said. That's how I knew I couldn't do it. Aiming that rifle at a human.

Richard appeared at the bottom of the stairway and shouted up at us in disgust, I guess he was never in 'Nam, was he? He looked away, blew out a stream of smoke, and threw open the front door of the dorm, leaving us to digest his contempt.

Later, we sat in wait at the top of the stairs for Richard to come back from lunch, and when he threw open the front door of the dorm, we let him have it from the second story with two of the fire extinguishers. They were all over the campus: large, silver, water-filled canisters. We shot him with a long, fierce, pressurized stream of water, making for a solid ambush. He was soaked, a clowning casualty long before he knew what hit him.

We left empty fire extinguishers all over the campus that summer, going back and forth, testing each other every way we could. We knew about consequences, but during those long, hot summer days, we seemed to be either too young or too old, and the truth was that none of us wanted to care.

Andrew Gottlieb lives in Irvine, California, and spends more time than he should letting fly-fishing get in the way of his writing. Remarkably, he now helps raise two teenagers. He prefers road trips to work of any sort. Find him at www.andrewcgottlieb.com.

A GHOST IN THE MALL

BY NATALIE SINGER-VELUSH

As much as the house I grew up in, the cars my parents drove,
the cold classrooms and school hallways I roamed for years—
as much as and more than these milieus, when I think of my
teenhood, I think of the mall.

I can see myself there now, standing at the end of the low
brown brick building, under a dull flickering fluorescent.

I have just walked through the glass doors near the entrance
to Eaton's, the Canadian department store where we bought our
socks and underwear and where, in its heyday as an upper-class
destination, my grandparents took me to lunch at the cafeteria. I
still feel the cheese lasagna steaming beneath my eager little face,
my Mary Janes knocking the post underneath the laminate table.

But now I am fourteen. It is snowing outside, the big
new flakes of another deep winter. My brown hair is frizzy,
my coat wide open. A plain gray school uniform is rumpled

underneath; my winter boots slush-stained. I walk with a couple of girlfriends, gossiping about boys or the bitchy geography teacher. But even as I nod and swear perfunctorily, I am fielding my own private thoughts.

We walk past the windows of the stores, Jacob, Roots, Mexx. I study the mannequins, who are wearing the kind of clothes that I don't own. They pose in their short black skirts, bomber jackets, Doc Martens. I cannot have these things, because they cost money my mother doesn't have.

I marvel at the mannequins' slender smoothness, their creamy unblemished robot skin. I am the opposite of them, me with my frumpy shirt from Reitman's, where the single mothers and cleaning ladies shop, where my own mother drags me when I desperately need something new and berates me. "What is wrong with this?" she urges, waving a polyester thing in my face. "You are so spoiled. Money doesn't grow on trees. And I don't see your father offering to buy you kids anything."

Carol and I talk about the weekend as we examine an ivory cable-knit sweater we've seen the rich girls wearing. "Can you sleep over Saturday?" I ask hopefully. Carol is also not popular, even though she has a thick, straight ponytail and married professor parents. When we hang out we sneak reads of her older sister's diary, steal from her younger sister's candy stash, and make prank calls to this really weird sex party line we discovered.

"I don't think my dad will let me," she says. Her parents keep her close to home.

"Fuck," I say.

When the mannequins and sweaters become too much, I turn my focus to the other groups of girls and boys our age roaming the grubby mall floor in little cliques. I pass right by some of them but they do not look, as though I am the air itself.

The girls defy their very DNA—they almost all attend the private Jewish day schools nearby. But they are crowned with shiny gold hair, glossy and neat down their backs or gathered in sexy/messy ponytails jutting out of their small, well-shaped heads. They wear uniforms too, but their skirts have sharp, black pleats, their tights patterned, their boots laced high. They have real diamonds in their ears and gold nameplates hanging down their necks.

These girls, who sometimes knock into me as they brush by, walk with boys. Beautiful, unreal boys with tousled hair and letter jackets and white teeth. Boys who put their arms around the girls and grip their small waists. Boys to whom I am invisible.

I stand in my gaping coat, studying the mall floor tiles as they move by, as though I have important business down there and my ears aren't burning red from the shame and irrelevance of my existence. This is how it is for me, how it always has been. I am fine—I look okay, not beautiful but not horrifically ugly, a little pimply but not covered from chin to forehead in fat blackheads like Andrea in homeroom. I know the prerequisites for fitting into the world around me—stylish clothes like the mannequins, lustrous hair, parents with vacation homes. But I don't have the key to get in. I can't get through those windows. I need to be perfect, I know that, but I can't.

So I walk with my other smart, funny, but also invisible friends through the mall, past the colored cement indoor playground where I scrambled as a child, past the deli where the ambling bubbies in their fur coats order challah and baba ghanoush, past the Cattleman's where we sometimes stop for wide golden steak fries stacked like thick pencils in oily paper cups.

The voices of the mall travel and echo like a train station, muffled, a sort of engine revving to take off. The thrum of the mall, and life outside its walls, moves past me. I stand in place feeling slightly drugged, unable to keep up with the action, the requirements. I think about the walk to my bus stop, the icy wait, the elegant houses I'll pass, the cracked steps that lead up to our sagging duplex.

Natalie Singer-Velush was born and half-raised in Montreal, Canada, before being uprooted and moved—at age sixteen—to the mythical, ice-cream-colored land of California, where she had to finish raising herself. There she discovered burritos, tried to become cool on the streets of San Francisco, and made out with lots of frogs before she finally found a prince. She's now a writer in Seattle.

A MOST DANGEROUS GAME

BY ALEXIS WIGGINS

You read the story in Mr. Trebor's class and guessed the ending before you got there. You remember the teacher's monotone voice almost made excited by the finale: The man hunts other men. You were bored. You chewed gum in your thirteen-year-old mouth and drew on your desk as Mr. Trebor read aloud.

That same year you and Marnie bought tight Lycra dresses at The Limited, bright tropical flowers blooming over your non-existent breasts. When your mother picked you up, Marnie's mom turned to her. "You have to see what the girls bought today," she said in a sing-songy voice that tried to be like bluebirds but was more like tin cans on pavement.

You tried on that dress at home in your bedroom, walked around in your mother's high heels and a stuffed bra, practicing. Practicing for a future that couldn't come any sooner.

When it came, you thought: only this? You thought maybe there was more. More than just grabbing and rubbing and shoving against each other in someone's parents' guest bedroom while the party thumped downstairs like a weak heartbeat.

And then you were out on your own, a big girl now. You were eighteen, but you felt thirty. You worked a night job, paid rent, and kept picking men up like stray cats. Or lint.

Antonio, a college boy who worked nights with you, let it be known with his wicked brown eyes that he wanted to fuck you. You let him think it might just happen, though you knew it never would. You let him walk you home some nights after work, let him come all the way to your apartment door and then left him there like a sweet fool. His wicked gazes at work made you flush, like catching glimpses of yourself in the Lycra dress from The Limited, wobbling back and forth in front of the full-length mirror.

One night in the basement warehouse, Antonio beckoned you with a finger: "Come here," it said coyly. For just one fluttering second you wondered what that finger would be like inside you.

You brushed him off, had work to do, but he insisted, pulled you by the hand—surprisingly soft—into a windowless room with a metal door that banged shut.

"There's nothing in here," you said, bored.

"Yes there is," he said, pointing to a dark corner. Your eyes grew accustomed to the low light, and you saw what was there: an old, stained sink. And before you could laugh at how dumb he was being, he put both hands on your shoulders, turned you around to face him, and breathed into your face, "Someday I'm gonna rape somebody." He paused, waiting for you to get it. "Maybe it'll be you."

You saw in his drill-bit eyes he wasn't kidding.

You spun out of there as if it were all a big, stupid joke. But inside you were trembling.

On the short walk home that night, you ran. You locked your apartment door with a loud thwack and took the phone off the hook. Crawling onto the old sofa in the dark, you remembered that story from Mr. Trebor's eighth-grade class. Only now, watching headlights flash across the bare wall, did you realize that you had been wrong about the ending.

It wasn't men who were hunted.

And you felt lighter-fluid flames of anger rise in you at the teacher who taught the wrong lesson. Or at the girl in the back row, in her cheap dress and scuffed heels, drawing hearts around boys' names, hoping.

Alexis Wiggins has been writing since she was five years old, when she wrote her first story, called The Lincoln Magic Penny; *it was written on her dad's typewriter and may have been the best thing she ever wrote. Alexis loves: reading, teaching teenagers, New York City, lemons, Spain, her hubby, and her two little boys. Alexis hates: the feeling of biting into peach fuzz, camping, mean people, and turbulence.*

THE CAUSEWAY

BY MARGARET MACINNIS

"Watch me, Margaret," my freckle-backed father said. Wearing cut-off Levi's and a silver crucifix, he stood barefoot on the cement wall designed to keep cars from driving off the causeway into the lake.

"I'm watching, Daddy."

"You have to stand up close to the wall and watch until my feet disappear." He was getting ready to dive into the "haunted" small side of the Whitins Reservoir. We—my younger sister and the cousins with whom we played—did not swim on the small side. Our mothers, aunts, godmothers, and grandmothers had so often recounted the stories of all-night searches for missing children, who later resurfaced, facedown and lifeless, that we would not have considered it. Not only was my father going to dive into this unfamiliar deepness, but he was going to swim under the causeway, through the pipe joining the two sides of the reservoir.

"Are you sure it's okay?" I pointed to the water. "Down there. In the pipe?"

"Yes," he assured me. "I've done this a million times. Don't worry about your old man."

Old man. He was not an old man. He was only thirty-two. Puppa, his father, was an old man.

"You're not old," I said, and he laughed at me.

"You take everything literally. No, I'm not old. But I have done this a million times. Relax." He smiled and patted my head. "You're such a worrier. Are you sure you're only eight years old? Look. Just wait until you can't see my feet anymore, cross to the other side, and watch for my head. Make sure you look both ways before you cross."

"When?" I asked.

"When what?"

"When did you do this a million times? Before you had me?" I wondered aloud, trying to piece together a portrait of my father as a young man right then and there, before I missed my chance, and he disappeared into his bedroom or backed down the driveway alone. Sometimes I would not see his face for days. That's just the way it was, but here in this moment, he was all mine. I had to make the most of it.

He sighed. "Yes, before I had you. Ask your mother. She's seen me do it. Mostly though, I did it when I was a kid. Twelve. Thirteen. Fourteen. Around then."

"Did your old man watch? Did Nanni?"

He guffawed, shaking his head at me. "Puppa and Nanni were nothing like me and your mother, nothing at all."

"What do you mean?" I wanted to know, oddly fascinated by the fact that my grandparents were almost strangers to me. We lived with my other "grandparents," Memé and Nana. Memé was my mother's mother, and Nana was Memé's aunt. At the time, I thought I knew all there was to know about them. My father's parents were the mystery.

"No more questions. I'm ready to go. On the count of three."

"On three or after three?" I asked, and my father groaned.

"Jesus, Margaret. Can I please go?"

Yes, I nodded, unable to speak, disappointment swelling in my throat. I had ruined everything.

He said again, "On the count of three. No, after three. Count." After making the sign of the cross, he arched forward into a diving pose.

"One, two..."

Splash. He must have meant on three. Down he swam. When I saw his feet vanish into the pipe, I ran to the other side without looking both ways. I was sure it was safe. Standing on the open causeway, you could see a car coming from a mile away. From the rocks that served as steps down to the water, I waited for him to surface. When he did, he looked dazed, almost as if he had forgotten where he was, who he was. "Daddy?" I reached out my hand and climbed down the rocks toward him. "Are you okay?" I asked as he grabbed my hand and pulled me toward him.

"Sure. Sure I'm okay." I clasped my hands behind his neck and felt the silver chain of his crucifix beneath my wrists. "I don't remember the pipe being that narrow. It felt like the walls were closing in," he said, gently pulling my hands apart and pushing me back toward the rocks where I could stand on my own.

Margaret MacInnis grew up in Massachusetts but now lives in Iowa City. Her essays about her parents and grandparents have been nominated for Pushcart Prizes and have been named Notable Essays in Best American Essays *and* Best-American Non-Required Reading. *She thinks everyone should tell their family stories.*

ORCHARD

BY KIM LOZANO

If the old woman knocked before the door opened, we didn't
hear it. Five teenagers and a manager, we'd all arrived early that
morning to work harvest at a Kansas grain elevator that rose
from the fields like a skyscraper. Wheat dust topped the 1980s
weather monitor that refreshed every few minutes, displaying
in miniature green squares the progression of rain toward our
spot on the map. Four pieces of duct tape formed a tic-tac-
toe pattern on the cracked vinyl cushion of the chair that sat
against the window overlooking the weighbridge of our testing
station. It was eleven o'clock at night and closing time. We kept
the elevator open as long as the wheat trucks kept coming, but
the evening dew made the wheat too tough to cut, and there
wouldn't be another truck until morning. One boy stretched
out on the couch with a wet rag draped over his itching eyes,
and the rest of us played gin rummy amidst an assortment of

candy wrappers, empty cans, and a Solo cup filled with tobacco juice.

We went silent as the woman moused in, hunched and lugging a large canvas bag. Everything about the tiny woman was brown—her pants, her homemade-looking blouse, her dirty Keds. She turned to shut the door, giving a hard push when it stuck.

"Do you have something to eat?" she asked. "I've walked a long way." I caught a glimpse of straight white teeth through her chapped lips.

I offered the woman a peanut butter and jelly sandwich, the safest bet from the fridge. She'd take two, she said. As my co-workers began clearing out, she settled herself at the end of the couch. I imagined her sleeping on the receiving platform attached to our building. We sat together until everyone but the manager had left, and without seeking consent from my parents and forgetting that my grandmother was in town, I asked her if she'd like to spend the night at my house. She hesitated and set down her Coke before accepting my offer.

I walked into the office, closed the door, and called my father to tell him that a woman had wandered up to our elevator and that I couldn't leave her, that I'd already invited her.

* * *

Her name was Cathy, and she rode back to town with me in my blue Grand Am. She said she used to be a schoolteacher in Bowling Green, Kentucky, and had stopped in at our grade school to see if they had any openings. She said that she walked at night to avoid problems with the police or anyone else who might harm her. When she saw headlights, she'd crouch in the ditch. She said she made her own clothes and brown looked nicest the longest. When I pulled into our driveway after the ten-minute drive, Cathy unfolded a handkerchief filled with apple seeds and held it in her lap for me to see. She was collecting them from every state she visited, she said, and when she finally settled somewhere she was going to plant an apple orchard.

My dad met us at the door and introduced himself. Behind him the living room sofa bed was freshly fitted with sheets and a pillow. The rest of the house was dark, and my family members were turned in for the night, although I felt sure they weren't sleeping. After showing Cathy to the bathroom, I returned to Dad, who was waiting for me in the kitchen. He reached into his pocket and pulled out a motel key. "Just a thought," he said. While Cathy and I were driving to town he'd gone to the small motel at the top of the street and reserved a room. We didn't have to offer it to her, he said, but if I thought she'd be more comfortable there we could. He held the key with its diamond-shaped keychain in the palm of his hand but kept it close to his own body, as if he already knew. I felt ashamed. For myself and for Cathy. I told him I couldn't ask her to leave. We could hear the sound of running bathwater down the hall. He put the key back in his pocket and touched my shoulder. "Okay," he said.

I made a pallet of quilts on the floor of the family room. I couldn't sleep. The familiar ticking of the grandfather clock rapped like a ruler on a desk. I thought about my family, awake in their beds. I thought about Cathy and wondered if anyone missed her, if she knew that everyone in the house was a little worried about what she might do. I lay awake staring at the ceiling's white popcorn surface.

***

When I got up the next morning, the sofa bed was put away and Cathy was sitting on the couch with her bag at her feet. Grandma sat by the window in the wing back chair, ankles crossed, rocking back and forth. She smiled and nodded toward Cathy. "Cathy's from Kentucky," she said, "and has quite a seed collection." Grandma proceeded to tell her about her own farmhouse in Oklahoma and how our family came down to see her every month.

"You ready, Cathy?" I asked. I wanted to pick up her bag and carry it, but it felt like some sort of trespass, so I didn't. We left early to get her to a town thirty miles down the highway and me on to the elevator. I was nervous to speak and afraid of not knowing what else to do to help her. Maybe I was afraid there wasn't anything else I wanted to do.

"You should write down your stories," was all I could think to say.

I dropped her off at a convenience store at the edge of town, knowing I'd never see her again. She hoisted her heavy sack out of the backseat and transferred it to her shoulder. She said thank you with a kind glance and shut the car door. I rolled down the window. I was embarrassed for not thinking about food before we left and for not bringing more money. "Cathy, you'll need some breakfast," I said and handed her ten dollars.

"I appreciate it," she said and turned and walked toward the store.

***

When I opened the front door that night, I found my mom sitting on the couch in her nightgown, her head leaning back on a pillow, eyes closed. I sat down beside her and gathered myself in the coolness of the velour couch. She placed her hand on my knee, and I rested my head against her. I knew to expect only kindness from my mother, yet I didn't speak, somehow afraid of her judgment. When I heard the whistle of the train across town, I rose to go to bed but then bent back down to give her a kiss, not sure what I was asking for.

I looked at her face, sleepy and serene.

"When I was a kid your Grandma took in a boy whose parents had moved away," she said without opening her eyes. "He stayed for a year."

"Thank you, Mom," I said.

Today, the sight of an old motel key or brown polyester pants will sometimes remind me of Cathy, or the wonder of an apple orchard.

Kim Lozano is a law school dropout who has five kids and wanderlust. She's an editor at a literary magazine and teaches creative writing to people over age fifty. Her poetry and prose have been published in The Iowa Review, Poetry Daily, *and elsewhere.*

WEIGHTLESS

BY STEVE BREZENOFF

Jake and I hadn't been friends in a long time, like not since middle school. Since then, he'd let his hair grow insanely long. He'd taken to working out and lifting weights. Back in middle school—and before that, when we'd been friends in grade school—he'd been sort of on the chubby side.

Now, in eleventh grade, Jake takes off his shirt at every minor provocation: warm day, basketball game, sunny lunchtime. Doesn't matter. Dude's shirt is coming off.

Meanwhile I've drifted into my own circle. I drink a little beer, smoke a little pot. But mostly, I'm a quiet kid—if there's a way to avoid standing out in a crowd, talking in class, or showing up at all, I'll find it.

So how it happens that Jake and I start hanging out again junior year, I can't really say, and though our rediscovered friendship (if that's what it is) doesn't last long, without it I wouldn't be at the party at Sam Mewz's house.

Sam Mewz, in the last four years, has become one of Jake's best friends—they both play instruments, and similar taste in music is about all it took to seal the deal. I play an instrument too. I play the trumpet. But the trumpet, in spite of its appearance in dozens of excellent rock songs of the 1960s and 1970s—not to mention every amazing soul record since the advent of the genre and easily seventy-five percent of the best jazz recordings of all time—is not the sort of instrument one plays in high school with long hair and no shirt. That sort of thing is reserved for three instruments: the guitar, the bass guitar, and the drums. All right and maybe the saxophone. Maybe keys. But that's it.

Jake plays the drums, and Sam plays the guitar—lead guitar. They've bonded over this shared ability to fill out a rock band, I suppose, and so they've become friends, jamming endlessly in Jake's basement. It is in Jake's basement, among his music equipment and free weights, that I find myself one Friday evening with Jake, Sam, and a couple of other guys (a bassist and a saxophonist). These guys know each other well, and though I'll still know Jake's birthday decades from now and can tell you dozens of inside jokes from seventh-grade science class and which *Calvin and Hobbes* strip is his favorite, I am definitely on the outside of this little group. But these guys are confident, popular, and seem to smile way more than I ever do, so I'm happy to hover at their periphery.

"When are they leaving?" says one of them—let's say the bassist, who is the tallest of the bunch, with the longest hair and the darkest sunglasses and the best-looking girlfriend.

"They should be gone by now," Sam says. "I'm supposed to be staying here all weekend." He giggles into his chest. For all his technical guitar prowess, Sam is still a giggler, like he was back in second grade when I met him. In fact, he's the certifiable class clown, which means everyone knows he exists. At least he talks, though, which is more than I can say.

"So let's head over there," says the saxophonist, with his head jutting out on his long neck, like an investigating turtle. He's been playing the sax for so many years, his neck is just kind of stuck like that.

"You coming, bro?" says Jake.

"To Sam's?" I say, though it's obvious.

"Yeah, man." He gets up from his throne and finds his shirt. "I told you about this, right?"

He didn't, but who cares anyway? "Sure. Okay."

"Cool," says one or all of them at the same time, and eventually the four of us step out into a crisp fall night, and make our way—through backyards and bushes—to the Mewz residence. A bunch of cars are already parked out front, and a gaggle of kids is gathered on the front lawn, waiting to get inside. Sam takes it in stride, giggling and greeting his guests. This is what we call an open house: it means a party to which everyone on God's green earth is welcome because the parents are out of town.

Now, this isn't my first open house party. I've dropped by at least five since I started high school, and I've sipped some very inexpensive beer. But this crew—this is not my normal crew. The kids piling into the Mewz house and backyard, though familiar, might as well be twenty-five exchange students from Ukraine.

That's not completely true. I know their names. They speak English. I've probably been in at least one class with like ninety percent of them. But we're not friends. We're not even friendly. And though I'm fairly comfortable with a little 420 and I'm happy to find a red plastic cup and nurse a light beer til the wee hours and I'll even fake my way through a couple of cigarettes in an evening if it's expected, that's about as far as my journey into the world of controlled substances goes.

Not so with this crew. Sam, our giggling host, has a little baggy of something he's calling Special K, though it doesn't look like any breakfast cereal I've ever seen. I overhear someone call it cat tranquilizer. I pass. I take my red plastic cup, fill it at the keg on the back deck, and find the sliding doors to the living room, where a handful of "partiers" are reclining slack-jawed in front of the TV. There's a cooler in the middle of the room, so when after a few minutes of nervous sipping I find my red cup empty, I grab a can and crack it open. The foam runs down the side and I slurp it up. Someone laughs, and for an instant my face goes hot, but then I realize they're not laughing at me.

A *Cheers* rerun is on, or something equally familiar and harmless. In fact, everything in the room—from the faux-leather sectional seating to the people on it—is familiar and harmless. Or maybe it's the beer. It gets kind of fuzzy. But for some reason, I'm feeling pretty good, pretty light—weightless, even. Right across from me on the U-shaped couch is Melanie Kize. She's beyond familiar and harmless: She's lived next door to me since I was two years old, and we probably took a bath together at least once.

I should be uncomfortable, away not only from my real friends—who aren't with-it enough to have heard about this open house—but even from my ersatz friends who don't like wearing shirts. I have nothing more than a passing acquaintance with any of the slack-jawed Special K users in this room. Even Melanie and I—though she smiled and waved when I came in and fell into the seat opposite her—haven't exchanged much more than a flaccid greeting in six years.

So I figure it must be the beer that's got me feeling carefree. Whatever it is, it has completely taken me over, and that's when the Gap ad comes on.

Let me back up. I mentioned earlier that seventy-five percent of the best jazz recordings of all time featured a trumpet. I stand by that. But James Moody was a saxophonist, and his version of "I'm in the Mood for Love" is legendary. Musical history. His improvised solo inspired lyrics even, and vocalist King Pleasure recorded them and made them a huge hit, which eventually became the audio track of a commercial for pants. The commercial was thirty seconds long, not nearly long enough for the whole track. But I loved the whole track, and I knew the whole track, every word, every vocal flare, by heart.

Back to the Mewzs' living room. We hum along, some of us. I know the words, so I sing. When the commercial ends, we stop. Except me. I keep going. I sing every word of the goddamn song, louder and louder over the next two commercials, till the uproarious finish. When it's over, I sip from my beer to find the TV's on mute and the eyes of the world are on me.

Melanie says, "Oh my god, what?"

Were they impressed? Repulsed? I don't know. I'll never know. But no one would ever forget I was at that party, as they did about my appearance at every other open house before or after. That's something in itself for a quiet guy, but what was more important, I think, was that weightlessness. It never went away, which is how I discovered it wasn't the beer. It was something bigger. Because though I don't know if they were impressed, repulsed, or merely confused, I do know I didn't care anymore, and that's where the weightlessness came from.

Steve Brezenoff is the author of the young adult novels Guy in Real Life, The Absolute Value of -1, *and* Brooklyn, Burning, *as well as dozens of chapter books for younger readers, including the Field Trip Mysteries and Ravens Pass series. He grew up on Long Island, spent his twenties in Brooklyn, and now lives in Minneapolis with his wife, Beth, who is also a writer for children, and their children, Sam and Etta.*

PART THREE:

LOVE
MADN

AFTER THE PARTY

BY GEOFF HERBACH

Yeah, it was 1987. Yeah, I lived in the hills of Southwest
Wisconsin. But no, I didn't drink. Almost every kid in my high
school poured it down. At the time, in that place, without the
Internet to lull us or cell phones to keep us hooked like the
unborn to our parents, that's what most of the kids did. They
got loaded.

I sort of wanted to do it—get hammered and make out,
or whatever (everybody had funny stories)—but I was scared.
Earlier in the school year a party had been narc'd off. In the
locker room, this freshman girl, Jenny, heard some senior girls
donkey laughing about a total blowout at the quarry and Jenny
took that info to the assistant principal. She named names. After
an investigation, several jock-girls lost their volleyball seasons
to a code infraction (thou shalt not drink wine coolers). So, I
was scared. I lived for sports.

***

On a Saturday in March, my pal Joe's parents took off to some
B&B in Mineral Point. Joe got on the horn. Bring beer, bring
wine. I have pretzels. The word spread fast. My girlfriend,
Maureen—oh man, I loved her: lip-gloss, shampoo, shoulders,
hips—she was psyched. Just a week earlier she'd complained
about how our friends never had any fun. Pretty much my
whole class went, including me. But no, I didn't drink. I
cleaned up spills, held the hair of the vomiting, drove people
to Kwik Trip for their cigarettes, and at the end of the night,
cleaned up all the party trash and loaded it in the backseat of
my Ford Fiesta for disposal.

There was only one job left: deposit the inebriated
Maureen at her house on the edge of town. She wanted to make
out. She wanted to fight. She loved me so much. She had to go
to sleep.

***

The freshman girl Jenny hadn't fared very well that year. A
senior donkey girl accused her of being the narc and she'd
admitted it. Crazy. I heard rumors. Tobacco spit on her locker,
car window broken with a big chunk of limestone, physical
threats, late-night phone calls, a crushed cat thrown on her

doorstep. I thought: Whoa, don't ever tattle up a group of wasted seniors. And that's pretty much all I thought.

* * *

Midnight. A light, wet snow fell. The road to Maureen's house curved into the rolling country. By our town's standards, that's where the rich lived (in the hills, in white split-levels, set back behind pine trees). Halfway down the road, in the dark, I pulled over, grabbed the bags of bottles and assorted party muck from the backseat of my car, and dumped it all in the ditch. Maureen shouted. The bottles made a lot of noise crashing, but I didn't worry. No one could possibly see me.

You know what? Maureen loved me so much. Then she got so mad. Then she had to go to sleep. I helped her to the door of her house then turned around to get myself home.

A third of the way back up the road I saw a small light dancing between snowflakes. I put on my brights to see. But I couldn't. Only the snow got brighter. My chest tightened. As I neared the source, the light went out and a dark figure emerged. It was a man, maybe in his forties. With his right hand he made a circular gesture telling me to roll down my window. I did. He stood next to the car. With his left hand he held up a bag of bottles.

My heart began to pound. Oh God. Thou shalt not transport empty booze bottles. Oh God.

"You?" The man blinked at me. "It's you?"

"Me?" I asked.

"You," he hissed. He reached into the bag and threw a bottle into the car. It crashed and shattered.

I screamed.

He threw another. It hit me on the cheekbone. I threw the car in reverse, spinning in snow, skidding away. He chased. When I stopped to swing the car around, to race off in the other direction, he stood in front of me, trapping me between himself and the steep ditch, the bag of bottles held over his head like a bludgeon he would crush through my windshield. He held steady. We stared. My heart sucked and blew in my chest. I thought: Run him down. But I didn't want to run him down.

He lowered the bag. I exhaled. I cried out my window, "I don't know what you're doing. What are you doing?"

He sagged. "My daughter is in there convulsing. She said it was you, but I couldn't believe it was you. I thought you were a good one."

"Please," I said. "I don't know what's going on."

"Breaking windows, killing animals. We thought it was rough kids. But if it's you? What are we going to do? If it's you, too?"

Then I remembered that the freshman Jenny lived on this road. I guess I knew she lived near the first big curve.

Her dad talked. "Do you want to kill her? Do you want my daughter dead?"

"No. I don't," I said. "I swear to God."

A minute later, I stood in front of her. Jenny was wrapped in a blanket. Her mom held her. Convulsing. That was the right description.

I knelt in front of her. I rambled. I'm sorry. I'm so sorry. Drove Maureen home. I don't drink. Trash. I couldn't keep it in my car. I wouldn't hurt anyone. I don't care about the donkey girls. Why would I care? I don't want you to hurt. I don't chew tobacco. I don't drink.

She looked at me, fisheyed, and shook. She nodded, or maybe it was involuntary, and I wanted to wrap her up, cover her up, make her know that she was safe, but she wasn't safe, and I was just this dumb kid so worried I'd lose my outdoor track season.

"Let's go," her dad said. I followed him back through the house and out onto the driveway. "If you have trash from a party, put it in a dumpster. Don't just ... " He stopped and exhaled. "Jesus. Screw it." Then he said, "Me and my family enjoyed watching you play football last fall."

"Oh. Okay. Thanks," I said.

"Screw it," he said again. He turned and walked back into his house.

For a moment, in that driveway, in the rich part of town, the snow falling, I thought, everything is a bad dream and everyone is stuck, and I just want everyone to be okay, I want to make everyone okay.

But I couldn't. And I didn't.

By June, I was at the quarry with the donkeys. And yeah, I did drink, like that was the only answer.

Geoff Herbach's young adult novels, Stupid Fast, Nothing Special, I'm with Stupid, *and* Fat Boy vs. The Cheerleaders, *have been listed in the year's best by many associations that seem to know what they're talking about. Prior to writing YA, he published a literary novel,* The Miracle Letters of T. Rimberg, *wrote comedic radio and stage shows, and traveled the country telling weird stories in rock clubs. He teaches creative writing at Minnesota State University, Mankato, and lives in a log cabin with a very tall wife named Steph.*

ON THE THIRD DAY

BY TOM MORAN

On my first day of high school, a good ten minutes after the bell had rung, a new kid came through the door of our Spanish class. As he passed by, Mr. Paez, our teacher, stopped mid-sentence and stared. We all did. Tall, skinny as a twig with a long Appalachian face and dark stubble that made him seem weary and a good four or five years older than the rest of us, the kid looked like Abraham Lincoln costumed to play a few of Brando's scenes in *The Wild One*. His white T-shirt was ironed and spotless, the sleeves rolled up like condoms to show off arms as thin as spaghetti strands. His unwashed Levi's were pulled down so far that only a death grip from a wide black belt kept the pants from falling off completely. The bottoms of the denims were tucked into polished black motorcycle boots, each with its own shiny chrome buckle. The boy's body danced as he walked down one of the aisles between desks, his limbs rolling this way and that, his head bobbing to the rhythm of some private music. He flopped into the seat across from me, sprawled his long legs out across the aisle, and winked.

His name was Phil Nicholson. Pale and fragile, it was hard not to grin at his biker garb and tough guy pose. That first day on campus he turned heads. By the second day the school's jocks, hoods, and surfers were calling Nicholson names and laughing at him, trying to see who could get deepest under his skin. On the third day just before the first bell, he snapped, pushing a football player, an all conference lineman who also held the school record for tossing a shot put, and by lunch break everyone on campus knew that when classes let out that afternoon the weird new kid would be stomped senseless in the alley behind school. It was the kind of train wreck no one wanted to miss.

Our proximity in class made Nicholson and me partners for Spanish practice, and he listened as I read phrases from *Hablar y Leer* and practiced rolling my r's. That Wednesday he showed no concern about his after school appointment. "Come have a look," he said. "You can be my second. *Mi segundo*." His pronunciation was near perfect.

I went. So did nearly everyone in school. The alley was jammed. I wasn't exactly Nicholson's second, but I was the only one who stood anywhere near him. His opponent wasn't much taller than Nicholson, but he was all body, a thick neck, knotty biceps, veins tunneled along massive forearms. His friends laughed and slapped the ball player on the back as he stepped into the center of the alley.

Nicholson nodded toward me, forced a grin, and then slowly walked out. There were titters throughout the crowd. All pale skin and bones, Nicholson seemed a clown, his pants sagging down below his ass, his boots at least two sizes too big for his frame. It was impossible to imagine him offering even the slightest challenge.

The jock snarled an obscenity and strode forward, his right fist cocked by his shoulder. Nicholson stood still, poised like a matador, waiting for the fist to be unleashed. When it was, Nicholson ducked and his right hand dropped to his ankle, his fingers reaching inside the top of his boot. He whipped out a long metal chain and it arced through the air. The chromed steel lashed across the jock's mouth, snapping teeth off the way a careening car levels highway road signs, a slurry of blood and white chips spewing into the alley. The jock's arms flew up to his face and he dropped to his knees, blood boiling from his mouth.

We were all stunned. The downed jock moaned and cried out in pain. Nicholson turned, the chain draped over his hand. Our eyes met briefly, and he shrugged. Then he began walking away. Several of the jock's friends shouted threats, but no one pursued Nicholson. He turned a corner and quickly disappeared.

My first year of high school had barely started, and standing in that alley it could not have been clearer that I had a lot to learn. That was a long time ago. I never saw Nicholson again.

Tom Moran spent much of his life in Southern California, where he wrote about the surfers, boardwalk entertainers, artists, and dreamers who lived and played at Venice Beach. He currently makes his home in upstate New York, where he has discovered that writing about his own days beside the California sand can help get him through the snowbound winters.

HOW TO SUCCEED BY ACTUALLY TRYING

BY DAYNA EVANS

Every year my report card said the same thing.

In robotic Scantron print, it would read DOES NOT MEET POTENTIAL beneath every subject I'd taken. One of the automated selections teachers could choose to add commentary to students' performances, DOES NOT MEET POTENTIAL was the reason I hid my report cards and grimaced at my teachers. After four years of seeing those words, they ironically became the reason I stopped meeting my potential.

Come on. I got four A's, a B+, and a C in math. I had to be meeting *someone's* potential or else I wouldn't have done that well. My mother was also dissatisfied with me when she'd find the pale-blue printouts hidden beneath stacks of brown-paper textbooks.

"Dayna, what is this about? You need to *try* harder," she'd say. "What a waste of a brain!"

"But I got A's!"

"Clearly your teachers think you could do better. Don't just skate by in life."

And that would be that. We used to have a deal that I'd get $5 for every A, and I'd spend the cash on ugly band T-shirts or juicy breakfast sandwiches, but by my senior year, my mom didn't even go near her wallet. She wanted me to work harder, whatever that meant.

* * *

Everyone gets senioritis. It's not a myth—it's a crippling reality. For someone who had spent eleven solid years surviving on charm, last-minute paper writing, and a good track record, I had senioritis before even registering for my final year's classes.

Two study halls? Sure, why not? AP Music Theory? Let's go ahead and take that pass/fail.

The one class that I was torn on and that I'd been told I'd "really enjoy" was AP Government. The teacher was one of our best, all of my friends were taking it, and I'd at least get to sleep in before the lessons on bureaucracy began at 11 a.m.

In a last-minute moment of laziness, I checked the box for Government—the one without the advancement placement prefix. With Mr. Jordan. I heard he was funny.

My final fall semester in high school would be spent half sleeping, a quarter in marching band, and the remainder with Mr. Jordan, in what I thought was my brilliant curtain call performance of How to Succeed Without Really Trying. I was nailing senior year and it hadn't even started.

* * *

When I walked into Mr. Jordan's classroom on the first day, there weren't many familiar faces. I was considered a "smart kid" by my extracurriculars alone. Mr. Jordan was the assistant football coach as well as our high school's beloved goof-around history teacher, so it was clear from the start that I was to be outnumbered by athletes and popular kids. When I sat down, two well-liked cheerleaders asked me if I was in the right classroom.

"Uh, yeah," I mumbled. "I'm trying to take it easy this year, you know, with …" They'd stopped listening, instead turning back to each other to giggle while I slumped low at my desk.

I had flashes of an AP European project my freshman year when I'd convinced an artsy friend to help me.

"This is a replica of the room where the royal Romanov family was executed by Yakov Yurovsky and his henchmen. We even cut out little bullet holes," I'd said to my classmates and my exhausted teacher. I then told the story of the executions with deliberately exaggerated detail, a premonition for my future in writing, perhaps, but a fairly low manipulation of the system. The project was supposed to be an analytical research project, not story hour. I was given a too-generous B+, a grade I always felt guilty about because, well, I didn't even paint the shoebox.

Mr. Jordan called roll and did his introductory speech.

"Understanding your government is an essential civic duty," he started, but I was already zoning out. *Looks like I've got three study halls this semester after all*, I thought.

* * *

The semester progressed as I'd expected. I put a lot of energy into band and gave government my lowest priority. I'd show up on time, take a few notes, close my eyes during Mr. Jordan's screenings of *Schoolhouse Rock*—which he insisted still held valid knowledge for students of any generation—and passively absorb information when I could.

About two months in, Mr. Jordan announced we'd be staging debates.

"As a way to appreciate and thoroughly understand the United States' historic supreme-court cases, you will be assigned partners to debate both sides of twelve different cases. Whether you believe in your side or not, you're expected to defend it with research, details, and facts. If you convince us, you'll do well."

The whole class groaned. Partner work at any age was a bore, but particularly as a senior.

Our pairs were assigned and packets were distributed, but nobody made an effort to acknowledge their partners.

I'd been assigned *Roe v. Wade*, a landmark case in the 1970s that legalized abortion in America. I was pleased: It was a case I had feelings about. I looked at the bottom of the sheet at my partner's name, and my excitement plummeted. I'd be debating *against* legalizing abortion. Josh Terry, our grade's class clown, would get the other side. I was indignant. And then things got worse.

Before we began preparations for the debate, Mr. Jordan gave us a pop quiz, something he'd never done before. "I want to make sure you've been doing your reading," he said. I hadn't been because I believed I would eventually, and so I was hard-pressed to find the answers. I turned in my blank quiz sheepishly.

***

At the end of the day, I was walking past Mr. Jordan's classroom and I proudly stomped in.

"Mr. Jordan, I need you to change my debate assignment," I said. "I cannot—and I mean, *cannot*—argue against legalizing abortion. It's not in my constitution, and I strongly believe in a woman's right to choose."

He sat at his desk, legs crossed and leaning back on his wooden swivel chair.

"Go on," he said, grinning.

"The government shouldn't have any hand in my—or any female's—body! There's an implication of church infecting state there, and I thought we were a country who didn't allow that."

"I see." He looked pleased, but he wasn't saying much.

"How am I supposed to argue that our government, which is run by mostly old white men, should tell women, under circumstances of rape, that they can't do what they want with their own uteruses? I can't! I really can't!" I was yelling now, slightly out of breath. Mr. Jordan turned away from me and reached into his desk for a yellow folder.

Abruptly, he handed me my quiz from earlier that day and said, "I failed you on your pop quiz."

I held the paper, its blank spots now dominated with red x's, and saw the giant F at the top.

"You haven't been doing the work," he said. "You think I haven't seen this before?"

"Uh, seen what?" I felt deflated after my passionate burst of energy.

"A smart kid who only wants to do the minimum amount of work to get by. If you just *tried* to invest, you'd be surprised at how much you'd get out of it. I'm not so easily bought by this 'whatever' attitude. You clearly believe in something."

I felt pangs of hot shame on my face. "Uh, I'll try harder, I guess."

"I'm not going to change your debate assignment," he said calmly. "If you want to come in here and have it all handed to you because you think your brains are enough, you're wrong. Prove to me that you know how to work hard."

To translate: Dayna, meet your potential.

***

The day of the debates, I was nervous. I'd spent endless long nights researching a position I didn't believe in, crafting the right words with which to deliver it, and finessing each counterpoint I could predict Josh would invoke. I wanted desperately to do well.

Josh and I spent two full weeks working on the debate and when I came up to the podium, I felt sturdy as a pillar. I wasn't a tremendous public speaker, but I felt I had persuasion and work to back me up. I was empowered by my commitment. He and I made it through without any severe hiccups, and the class clapped heartily.

At the end of the following week, Mr. Jordan passed back notes on our debates, as well as our grades, and I stalled before turning mine over. I hadn't recovered from the unfamiliar red-lettered F from a few weeks before.

When I did, however, I was thrilled. A-. In his note to me, Mr. Jordan said he'd have given me an A if I had crisply responded to Josh's point on right to privacy, where I'd waffled.

"Imagine if you'd debated the side you were passionate about," he'd written. "Great job."

I turned the page over again, and it felt as heavy as a trophy.

Dayna Evans is a writer from Philadelphia who moved to New York when she was seventeen. She likes to eat doughnuts and travel, best of all when these things happen at the same time.

TEN YEARS AGO

BY SARAH BETH CHILDERS

Senior year. A fundamentalist Baptist high school. One of those times, frequent and interminable, when the teachers ran out of lesson plans and gave us time to talk. I was reading a novel because I'd run out of homework.

The classroom chatter softened for a moment, and I heard a nasal twang, four plastic chairs away. I stared at my book without seeing and focused my body on listening. Besides the nasal twang, Nick had basketball muscles, messy gelled hair, bright blue eyes, and, I thought then, the soul of a poet. Since I adored him, I believed our destinies were linked. Any word he said might affect me.

Nick's voice floated across the desks and sweaters as a wordless dragonfly whine, but I caught one complete sentence. "Yeah, that happened ten years ago," he said, his voice loud and serious. Those years sounded important, worth a boast. I looked up and saw he was talking to Heather. She'd slipped from her assigned seat in front me into the seat in front of him. The seat beside Nick was empty, but the seat in front allowed her to twist around and drape her arms and breasts across his desk.

"Ten years ago, huh?" Heather said, leaning her lavender dress closer.

Nick grinned and spoke again, but I'd quit listening. I'd quit wishing I was the kind of girl who never read novels and rested my breasts on Nick's desk. I felt as important as the girls in my class who got up at five to curl their hair, the boys who thought too often about their shoes. Ten years ago. We were old enough to say it. Like our teachers, like our parents, we could toss off a decade when telling a story. Oh, that was ten years ago now.

Never mind that ten years ago, downstairs in this same brick building, I'd kept caterpillars in my desk tissue box and fed them leaves and crumbs from my sandwich. Nick had sported a haircut we called a "spike," short on the sides and topped with towering gelled sticks. After he'd sweated his hair flat at recess, he'd slip into the boys' restroom to add more gel. "My mom says my hair makes me look like a rock star," he'd said, flashing a half-baby-teeth grin.

Ten years ago, I hadn't met Heather, but my mom had seen her once in a grocery store checkout line. Heather's father, a short man in a professionally pressed white shirt, had pushed the shopping cart, and Heather, all hair bows and lace, had stood beside him, her fingers locked in the side of the cart. She'd removed one hand and pointed at a roll of powdered donuts, and her father had slapped her. But the reality of our decade was irrelevant. We were eighteen, with ten remembered years behind us, and to me, this felt like the definition of adulthood.

The bell rang, and I hurried past my classmates and downstairs for my most significant social interaction of the day: My third-grade brother met me between my classes by the little boys' bathroom. "Hi, Sarbef!" Joshua yelled, his hazel eyes big with surprise, as if we'd both happened by. Then he told me the kindergarteners had played in the urinals that morning, and the elderly janitor had chased him with a mop.

Running back upstairs, sliding into another plastic chair for another class, I couldn't imagine how it would feel to speak even of twenty years ago. When Nick would be too fat to look like a Christian rock star, but he'd be one, preaching the evils of Christmas trees from his Facebook pulpit. When Heather would be divorced with four cats, sewing her own clothing and brewing laundry detergent. When I'd sometimes run short on my own lesson plans, and my little brother would be dead.

At eighteen, life was as light, changeable, and as full of possibility as the dolls I had cut from notebook paper at eight. Add crayon green scrubs and a stethoscope and I'd be a doctor. Add a couple of paper kids and I'd be a mom.

I didn't know yet that years had weight. I could carry my

past behind me like a kite, each moment adding ribbons to my string.

Sarah Beth Childers went to a tiny Christian school in Huntington, West Virginia, where she played basketball but never made a shot, ran track but never won a race, and played an old British woman who got strangled in a high school play. She now lives in Richmond, Indiana, where her cat pulled down the living room curtains so she could get a better view of passing cars and her Boston terrier pried open a gap in the fence so she could play with the dog next door. Sarah Beth wrote about her and her mom's teenage years in her memoir, Shake Terribly the Earth: Stories from an Appalachian Family.

END OF THE HALF

BY PATRICK HUELLER

Coach Hanson, my tenth grade basketball coach, was angry.

So angry, his words slurred together.

So angry, his spit speckled the floor.

It was halftime, and we were losing.

Again.

Two weeks earlier he'd told us our problem was that we didn't make enough easy shots. We spent that week shooting layups and free throws. When that didn't work, he blamed our conditioning. He locked away the basketballs and told us to line up at the baseline. We ran wind sprints until our bodies tingled with exhaustion.

At this point, I think Coach was out of ideas.

And the only thing he could think to do was yell.

When that didn't work, he tried yelling louder.

It was a home game, which meant we were in the weight

room. Coach Hanson liked to give the away team our locker room—to be a good host, I guess. My teammates and I sat on the benches of workout stations, staring at our feet. The floor was made up of black rubber squares that had been put together like puzzle pieces.

There was nothing to do but wait for Coach to stop shouting. This may have been the loudest of Coach's conniptions, but it wasn't the first. Earlier, his tirades had seemed more impressive. After all, the guy was almost seven feet tall! He'd played college ball! He could dunk! But at some point, as the losses piled up, it had become difficult to take him or his meltdowns seriously. (Of course he could dunk; he was almost seven feet tall!)

Coach could yell as long as he wanted; we knew we were still going to lose the game. Just as we had lost the last one, and the one before that, and the one before that. X's and O's seemed useless; defeat, inevitable.

There was definitely nothing I could do about it.

Not from the end of the bench—which, for the first time in my basketball-playing career, was where I sat every minute of every game. Blame it on a coach who was seven feet tall and couldn't understand the value of a classic point guard; blame it on the growth spurt that never happened; blame it on both. (I did.) For me, the only difference between halftime and the rest of the game was which bench I sat on.

CRACK!

By the time I looked up, Coach Hanson had already

broken his clipboard over his knee. It was a standard coaching clipboard—the dry-erase kind with the lines of a basketball court on it—or at least it had been. Now it was just two jagged pieces of plastic.

Coach wasn't screaming anymore. He was studying the wreckage in his hands.

You could see it dawning across his face: Without his clipboard, he wasn't going to be able to draw up any plays. Which made him even angrier.

He slammed the pieces of the clipboard against the floor. Anyway, he tried to. The floor was rubber, so the pieces didn't so much slam as harmlessly bounce. Which made him even angrier.

All at once he stormed, one epic stride after another, across the room. That's when—just before slamming the door shut behind him, just before deserting us in the weight room—Coach Hanson did a truly curious thing: He flipped off the lights.

Was it just a matter of habit—the result of a lifetime of turning off lights when leaving rooms? The guy was in a rage, so expecting logic was likely expecting too much.

Maybe Coach was trying to tell us something—something he'd been trying to convey all season long, with little success. Maybe he'd finally decided that words weren't enough. Maybe he was trying to show us that we'd been playing in darkness—and that it was time, at long last, to come roaring into the light. Maybe.

It's a cool thought, anyway.

Then again, if that's why he did it, he clearly hadn't thought the metaphor through. Because the darkness wasn't our only problem; we also had metal objects to navigate. Objects that were wide enough to jab and heavy enough to crush.

Which meant we didn't, we couldn't, roar into the light.

We had to tiptoe into it.

Single file.

With one arm I covered my dilated pupils; with the other I held on to the jersey of the guy in front of me.

The other team must have been at the other end of the court warming up. I could hear the screech of their sneakers. Coach Hanson? He, too, must have been close by. But I wasn't looking at him. I wasn't looking at any of them. I stood there, at the edge of the court, squinting at the gleaming asymmetry of the parquet floor, waiting for my eyes to adjust.

Patrick Hueller always assumed he'd grow up to be a sports star. One problem: He never actually grew up. Not literally. Not yet. He may be in his thirties now, but part of him still believes that he's going to wake up someday soon and be 6-foot-3. Until then, he'll continue to pursue his backup plan of writing books. One of those books is Foul*, a horror-sports novel (written under the pen name "Paul Hoblin"). Another (as "P. W. Hueller") is* Wolf High*. That one's got sports in it, too. And werewolves.*

SUSPENDED

BY KYLE MINOR

The locker room walls were painted puke green and lined like a cage with metal hooks, and red mesh equipment bags hung from the hooks like meat. One of the bags was swinging, and I was swinging in it, and Drew McKinnick slapped at it and did his punching, and the janitor got me down.

What did my father say to the principal, and how many times had he said how many things? My boy is not eighty pounds yet. My boy is in the seventh grade. My boy is not a linebacker. Can't you see I love my boy? If you had a boy to love what would you not do?

What did the principal say to my father? Did he say he had a boy and the boy got caught drinking in the tenth grade and he kicked his own boy out of school, same as anybody else? Did he tell my father what he told us once a year when they brought

the boys into the gymnasium and left the girls away? I loved
and love my wife, and she is not my ex-wife, not praise Jesus in
the eyes of God, despite her running off with the Navy captain,
despite it all I wait and wait and one day she will be restored to
me. I know it in my heart of faith, I wait as Hosea waited, now
let us pray.

Whatever passed or did not pass between them, this once
it did not matter how much money McKinnick's father gave the
school, or how many animals he had veterinaried to health, or
how many ordinances he had sealed with his mayor's seal. This
once I came home beaten and bruised and told my father, "They
suspended him for three days."

That night I slept and dreamt of three days free of red
ears flicked blood red and slapped until I heard the ocean. The
bathroom was mine to piss in, free of fear of footsteps from
behind, one hand in my hair and the other on my belt, the
painful lifting, then my head beneath the commode water.

That afternoon I skip-stepped to the bus, the Florida sun
high and hot, and this once thinking the heat balmy and tropical
rather than stalking and oppressive. Then, somewhere between
the Route 7 and the Route 8, somebody grabbed me by the
collar and slammed me against the black bumper. At first I
thought it was him, because it looked like him, same dogteeth,
same mocking smile, but bigger somehow, and how had it been
kept from me he had an older brother?

"You think you're something," he said, and lifted me until
my feet were off the ground. He was as big as my father. "You

ever run crying on my brother again, I'll beat you within an inch of your life, you hear me? I wouldn't mind breaking you."

He had me up against the back of the bus, and somewhere somebody had taught him how to do it, and his brother, too. I can see their faces now, but younger, fleshier, their father pressing their bodies to the wall, and then, older, leaner, their sons looking down at their fathers in their fear, learning.

Kyle Minor lives in Indiana with his wife and two sons. His most recent TV series was not picked up by a network. His most recent book is Praying Drunk, *a collection of short fiction.*

GIRL/THING

BY ANNA VODICKA

Because I needed the cash, because it seemed like the girl thing to do, I took a certification course in babysitting to learn the essentials of diaper changing, of getting a baby to take the Gerber's off the spoon, and of infant CPR, which we practiced on naked, rubbery dolls. But they didn't teach us what to do when the job is done—when the littlest one, who screamed all night, is finally asleep in the crib, and the baby's father drives you home slurry at the wheel, and he slides a roving hand across the divide and onto the space that used to be known, seconds ago, as your innocuous upper thigh. "You're growing up so fast," he says. And sitting in the car—now a vehicle for ugly things like upper thighs, glassy eyes, and the rot-breath of intoxication—you think about how bullshit this all is, that you're growing up at the same rate as every other goddamned girl in that babysitting class who paid twenty-five bucks to have adults critique her in the art of child-rearing. A certified screw. But you can't do anything, because they've already taken your money, and this man is at the wheel, and your body is changing fast, so fast you don't know anymore if you are a girl, and if that noun means you are a person, place, or thing.

Anna Vodicka grew up in northern Wisconsin and has lived in Spain, South America, Palau (try finding it on a map), and many other parts of the world since. Before becoming a writer, she took on other roles to earn a living: English teacher, house painter, singer in the streets of Paris. She misses Wisconsin. She does not, however, miss babysitting.

SAYING GOODBYE TO ANNA

BY JACKIE BUCKLE

When you were fifteen, you did this quiz at school with some friends. It wasn't really a quiz, more like a game. You drew a grid and put your names at the top. Down the side of the grid were things like Hair, Smile, Personality, Legs. The idea was that everyone would anonymously rank the person's traits out of 10. Then you'd share the grids and have a good laugh because obviously it wasn't meant to be taken seriously.

That evening you threw up your dinner.

On purpose.

If we're being honest, the fact that you scored an average of 3 for your legs didn't give you an eating disorder overnight. There had been other things—like the throwaway comment that you had "the Tyler legs," or your teacher's observation that you'd make a great rugby player. And then there were the girls in the fashion magazines and websites. They didn't look like they'd excel at contact sports. They looked like they'd be blown away by a mosquito fart. That's what you said, and yet you wanted to look like that too.

So you went on a diet.

Again.

You'd been on lots of diets before, but there was this problem. You liked food—A LOT! And so the diets never lasted long. This time, though, you were determined. You would lose the weight if it killed you. You were tired of feeling useless and powerless. Now, for the first time ever, you felt you were taking control.

And so began your strange relationship with eating. Although you rarely made yourself sick, you would hide food all over your bedroom: in the cardboard tubes of used toilet paper rolls, behind your chest of drawers, even in old shoes. You weighed yourself every day, and when someone happened to comment that you seemed to be looking thin, it was like winning the lottery. You realized you were good at this. This was something you could do really well.

It is now nine months later. We are sitting in a small, anonymous-looking room, opposite Kelly the mental health nurse. If you don't put on weight soon you will spend the whole of the spring and summer in hospital.

"I said she had the Tyler legs."

Kelly provides a tissue.

Your legs are thin now. And yet, when you look in the mirror, you still aren't satisfied. "If I could just lose that last bit of flab on the calves," you say. But if you lose any more you'll end up as an inpatient being forced to eat, and the thought of that makes you frightened and angry. "Why do I have to be here at this stupid clinic?" you cry. "Why can't everyone just leave me alone?"

When you were little you dreamed that you would be a vet one day. You have always loved animals, perhaps because they never judge you. Animals don't tell you that you are too fat or too thin. Of course, you have to be smart to be a vet, but that was okay since you were getting straight A's. Now, with your poor school attendance, your grades have fallen.

You know that your anorexia—Anna, as you call it—is stopping you achieving things and sometimes you hate her for it. But at the beginning, Anna helped you. She may even have saved your life. She gave control to what felt like an out-of-control life. You were adrift in a torrent of emotion and believed Anna to be a strong, sturdy branch overhanging the river that you could grab onto. You felt safe. Now you don't know how to let go of her. Even though help is on the banks holding out its hand, beckoning you. You can't make the leap. It's like you have to keep hold of the branch or you might drown.

Another week goes by, and you don't put on weight. Kelly's face visibly sags as you step off the scales. "The same," she says, deadpan, and you take a long shuddery sigh—relief or disappointment? Kelly says she'll book an appointment with the hospital so you can see where you'll be staying.

Back home, the school must be phoned to let them know you'll be taking four months out, maybe more. It is a difficult call to make.

"I'm just going for a bath, Mum," you call.

You are cold all the time now, even in May when most people are in T-shirts. You often take a bath just to warm up, but what if you collapse? What if you have a heart attack? Will you be okay?

You say you are fine, but you aren't.

After your bath, you sit on your bed. You say you are tired of looking and feeling like this. That Anna has worn you out, and you can't let her do it any longer. You have made lists of the good and bad things about Anna. You know they are nearly all bad, and yet …

There are some pencils and a spiral notepad on your bedside cabinet, and you start to draw out a grid. Down one side you write: Compassion, Determination, Courage, Understanding. You put a 10 in every box.

You have three days before your final weigh-in. Three days to put on half a kilo, which is the very minimum you need to gain in order to stay at home.

You close your eyes and whisper, "Goodbye Anna," before we head downstairs together to the kitchen.

Jackie Buckle lives in England and is author of Half My Facebook Friends Are Ferrets. *She doesn't have a ferret but would like one. She does have two slightly crazy teenage daughters and an even crazier big furry dog.*

THE CATCH

BY MELISSA CISTARO

By the time they slid out of the cooler and onto our front porch, the ice surrounding their slippery bodies was nearly melted.

"Six silver Steelhead. Fresh out of the Klamath River," announced my mother.

They were sterling, pewter, and black. Yellow-eyed and long as my legs.

My mother pulled out a buckhorn knife and made a line, clean and silent, across the soft belly. A drop of rich red splattered between her pink toenails. She shoved the knife in deeper. I heard the sound of thin bones snapping like taut strings, the steel point of the knife scraping along a fine backbone. Her fingers, full of turquoise rings, yanked at things inside of the fish.

I was afraid of her. She wasn't predictable when she was drinking.

"Look at these," she said to me.

In her hand she held out three round fleshy balls. I winced. She pushed them closer to my face. They were like antique marbles, giant freshwater pearls—rare eggs with deep green and creamy swirls. They glistened in her palm.

"Aren't these amazing?" she said, squeezing my arm. I didn't want to touch them. And then I did. Fish guts. Soft, wobbly, and wet.

Perhaps now, so many seasons later, and her gone, I understand it better.

It was my mother who taught me beauty could exist in anything.

Melissa Cistaro is a writer and bookseller at the legendary bookstore Book Passage in Marin County, California. Writing is the only way she has been able to make sense of her world—both past and present. She has written a memoir: Pieces of My Mother.

THE WORLD IN A STUMP

BY WILL WEAVER

Sit long enough in one place, and the whole world will pass by.
—Chinese philosopher

It was the opening morning of deer season. My father and I stepped out of the house into black dark. No stars. He paused to puff out a breath, like a smoker exhaling, into the chilly November air. "South breeze," he said, "perfect for your stand."

I couldn't wait to get going. I had shot my first deer last year, when I was thirteen, but this season was different. I had earned the right to hunt by myself. Well, not entirely by myself. But at least I wouldn't have to sit in a stand with my father; he would be just down the trail and over a hill.

We rode in the pickup a mile beyond our farm to my grandfather's big woods. My father extinguished the headlights well before we stopped. Getting out of the truck, I eased shut my door with a muffled click. I carefully uncased my rifle, then shouldered my canvas Duluth pack, which contained lunch for all day.

"Ready?" my father whispered.

I quickly nodded, then followed his blaze-orange shape down the trail.

After fifteen minutes, he halted at a fork in the logging trail. He turned to face me. "Well, here we are," he whispered.

"Okay! See you!" I replied. I was in a hurry to get to my stand. His teeth gleamed white; he was smiling.

"Remember: sunup to sundown. If you can last the whole day on your stand, you'll see a nice buck."

I nodded impatiently.

"Think you can stick it out that long?" he asked. There was faint teasing—and also a challenge in his voice.

"Sure," I said, annoyed.

He put a finger to his lips. "Okay. I won't come for you unless I hear you shoot—and I don't expect to see you either."

I headed down the path. In my mind, I was already a mighty hunter. In summer, pesky ground squirrels, the kind that left dangerous holes in my father's cow pasture, disappeared when I showed up with my little .22 rifle. In October, ruffed grouse, or partridge, were fair game behind our farm on the trails among aspen trees. Carrying a sandwich and my stubby twenty-gauge shotgun, I ranged for miles across farm fields, around sloughs, and down logging trails. I was always on the move, always alert. Nothing escaped my eyes—especially deer sign.

My goal this season was to bag a giant buck. I had a great spot—thirty yards from a deer trail, muddy and torn up with use. The "stand" was a ground blind, a tree stump actually, with a half-circle of brush in front to keep me hidden from any passing deer.

Quickly I put down my seat cushion and placed my Duluth pack within reach. Checking the safety on my rifle, I turned to face the blue-black woods.

Six a.m. Not legal shooting time for another half hour. I sat rock still, as did the forest critters: They knew a stranger was in their midst. As long minutes passed, my heartbeat slowed, and the forest gradually came alive. A squirrel's feet skittered on oak bark. An invisible flock of diver ducks arrowed overhead, wings whistling. A partridge thrummed down from his night roost; the thwappity-thwap of his wings marked the path of his invisible glide through small poplars and brush.

At 6:20 a.m. blue darkness drained away. I could now see the deer trail, a darker ribbon through the woods. I shifted my boots—and beneath them a twig snapped. A deer crashed away behind me! My heartbeat raced to high speed. The deer had either been there all along—bedded down and listening to me—or else it had been coming along the trail. I couldn't believe my bad luck. In the distance, too far away to be my father's rifle, gunshots boomed here and there.

By the time I got over feeling sorry for myself, the woods began to open its curtains. Rusty-brown color seeped into the oak leaves. The grayness lifted—which meant the best half-hour for hunting was over. Disappointed, I leaned back on my stump.

At 9 a.m. I was shivering cold and had to stand up. The woods were brighter now, and quiet. Even the squirrels had stopped chattering and chasing each other. I drank a cup of hot cocoa. Old hunters joke that a sure way to see a deer is to put down your rifle in order eat lunch or take a pee. I tried both tricks. Neither worked.

After a snack, my short night of sleep caught up with me. Leaning back against a heavy limb, I blinked and blinked to stay awake. Once, my head slumped. The trail tilted and the oak trees tipped sideways; I shook my head to clear it. Then I let my eyes droop shut for just a second. When I opened them, there was drool on my chin. Several minutes had passed. My heartbeat raced again—but luckily there was no monster buck waving his white tail at me.

By noon I was restless. I considered walking up trail to check for fresh tracks—maybe a buck had passed during my nap—but I fought off the urge. I considered making up some excuse to check on my father. Instead, I occupied myself by doing housekeeping on my ground blind. I made sure that there were no twigs anywhere near my boots. I rearranged its branches just right. This took all of ten minutes.

At 1 p.m. I stood up to stretch. My seat cushion fell off the stump, which gave me something new to do: Count the tree rings. As wide as a kitchen chair, the big pine stump had 83 rings, one for each year. The rings expanded outward, like a galaxy, like a universe. Ring number twelve had a dent—some old injury to the tree—perhaps a buck's scrape when the tree was small. I sat down again and refocused my eyes on the trail.

By 3 p.m. I was stir-crazy. What would it hurt if I got up and did some walking, some sneak-hunting? Maybe I could push a deer past my father's stand. How about a quick trek back to the truck to check out the field? Any place had to be better than here. But a promise was a promise. I stood up and did toe-raises until my calves hurt.

A few minutes after 4 p.m., something happened. The light was suddenly flatter, duller. The air was heavier, and still. A chickadee pecked and fluttered behind me, landing on my cap for a moment before moving on. The woods were waking up again. A partridge fluttered somewhere close. Squirrels scampered limb to limb. The trees stood straighter, more erect. As the fading light flattened to grays and blues, my hearing expanded. I heard the faintest sounds—a mouse in the grass, the peck of a nuthatch. What I couldn't see or hear, I felt.

At about 4:30 p.m. (I didn't dare look down at my watch for fear that I'd miss something), I turned my head slowly to the left. A deer materialized, as I knew it would! A small doe nibbled her way along, bobbing her head, twitching her tail. She was too small to take on the first day of the season. And anyway, I wanted to wait for a monster buck. But I was thrilled.

It was enough to have been looking in the right direction—to have been ready.

Light faded, pushed up the tree trunks and into the graying sky, as darkness gathered at ground level. For a few short minutes—the tipping point between light and dark at day's end—anything felt possible.

But the big buck never came. Shooting light was suddenly gone. I unloaded my rifle, secured the clip. Only a couple minutes later, my father appeared, a blob of orange moving slowly forward in the grayness. I stood to meet him and waved like a kid, though I no longer felt like one.

Will Weaver was born in Minnesota farm country. In college, by having too much fun and not paying attention, he accidentally became an English major. Since there was no escape from good books, he was forced to become an author. Of his many novels, his personal favorite is Memory Boy.

MOSQUITO MAN

BY DA CHEN

When the Mosquito Man comes to our village, I always smile, for he is our only storyteller. Every night under a tall tree, the moon shines with the sea breeze singing, some birds sleeping, some chirping. The mountains to the west cast shadows long and ghostly, and all the villagers gather around him.

Our Mosquito Man—he isn't made of mosquitoes or the emperor of mosquitoes. He is only a blind man. He sits under the tallest and hairiest pine tree. He drinks hot and steaming tea. Summer's evening heat is still burning. He waves his arms. He raises his hands. His voice rises and falls. He stands up. He dodges his proud head.

In the summer warmth, he wears no shirt, just simple shorts wrapping around his thin waist, as do I and all the village boys and men. We are the summer people—shirtless and barefoot. No heat can burn our feet. No shine can hurt our bared backs. We tan like slippery eels gliding in the shallow sea and darken like old turtles.

His tales are about lore, about our ancestry, about our battles won and lost, about our love, our hatred, about our tears and laughter, about our sea in which we plunge, about our mountains that we climb, about fathers lost in a tempest, about mothers crying over their widowhood, about ships that return and boats that do not, about the bumper harvest of the Moon Festival, about rich catches coming home at moonrise. He is the keeper of our past, of our present, of our songs, of our words, of our dialects, of the yearnings and musings of our dreams and laments.

As he tells us these stories, he wildly gestures. Sweat swings off his arms and back, his skin turns sticky, and mosquitoes land on him, making him a Mosquito Man. The lantern shining at his side shows motile shadows.

Village mothers bare their breasts to feed infants cradled in their arms. Babies no longer cry of hunger. The young ones yawn, and their mothers doze off, too.

Village fathers sit on bamboo stools smoking and sipping their hot jasmine tea. Fans in their hands chase away the swarms of mosquitoes brought here by the Mosquito Man. The fathers, too, doze off. After all, the day in the rice field has been long— cutting rice stalks in knee-high mud with field rats rampant, the sun biting, the cows stubborn.

The Mosquito Man stops suddenly the telling of his sweet tales as mosquitoes bite him, always when the story reaches its most interesting part. He slaps his palms over his back and shoulders blindly, for blind he is. My mouth hangs open, my black eyes cavernous. My breath seizes in my throat, waiting for him to continue, but he will not continue until all the mosquitoes are slapped away. The way he slaps, it will take a thousand years or more. So I sit next to him with a big palm leaf ready in my hand to keep the mosquitoes and moths away so he can tell his tales late into the yawning night until the moon looks tired and the stars cease to blink.

I sit by him, night after night, and tend to other things he might need. If his mouth gets dry, words stick and his tongue rolls not as slippery as before, and his lips smack with effort. His Adam's apple bobs up and down like a fist trapped in his throat, and he rolls his sunken eye sockets, two shallow holes without eyeballs. I know what to do.

I pick up his jug, a wooden one so it won't break if it falls, and run around the rows and rings of village fathers, asking them to spare some tea for the Mosquito Man. Some abide, others do not. I hit those heads with my knuckle, reminding them not to be miserly, and then I come back to our Mosquito Man with his jug full of tea. His trembling hands feel in the air, grabbing it readily, though uncertainly. He drinks loudly and gratefully, swallowing with the aid of his big Adam's apple. A peaceful expression crosses his wrinkled face. Then he says, as he often does when beginning a new tale, "I would not lie to you, my foolish listeners, for this is the truth, and I am only telling you all the truest version of it …"

He walks from village to village to tell the same tales. No one knows where he gets his tales. Possibly from another blind man, also surrounded by mosquitoes, with a boy like me fanning him to keep the insects away.

One day he simply stops coming to our village. No one knows where our Mosquito Man has faded to. Now I am the storyteller. I climb up a tall tree, followed by my good friends who love hearing my stories, who love the way I tell the stories, and the way I always begin by saying, "I am telling you only the true stories, nothing but the truth …"

I always sit on the easiest branch, with a cushy fork for my bottom and limbs to rest my feet upon. My young friends perch on other tree branches shaded by leaves and fruits. Though the blind man is gone, the mosquitoes are still here, biting my sour skin. Now I am the Mosquito Man, and a little boy with a big head and skinny body is fanning me with a palm leaf. His big eyes glint like gleaming caves, eager for the tales coming off my slippery tongue.

Da Chen is a New York Times *bestselling author. He's published seven books, including* Colors of the Mountain, China's Son, *and* Wandering Warrior. *Da was born in a tiny village in Southern China. He now lives in southern California, where he also writes TV shows and film scripts. Daily he runs on the beautiful beach and swims in the sea.*

PART FOUR

LOVE

APOLO

WARRIOR

BY TRISHA SPEED SHASKAN

As the summer sun warms my skin, I drop my McGill
skateboard onto the driveway and ride off, the wheels clattering
in a rhythm as steady as the crash of waves onto shore, washing
away everything that surrounds me—from the shadowed arms
of the large oak to the smell of fresh-cut grass. And I don't
think about being the only girl skater in this town because
the wheels clatter on. Or how my paisley shorts bunch up
in the crotch. Or how I sewed the shorts myself because in
Home Ec class the girls were only taught to sew sundresses,
which I obviously didn't wear. And I don't think about how my
hairstyle, one side shaved off from the part down and the other
side straight and shoulder-length, is another DIY job, or how
the friend who helped accidentally left a dime-sized bald spot
on my scalp. I'm listening to the sound of the wheels as they
clatter on. And what they tell me is: My hair and my shorts and
my board work and I work.

At fourteen years old, I count on this McGill—a sick hot pink deck that has a white skull at the center and a green snake twisting around it—to be my wheels. And when I'm on it, I can go wherever I want. Down the street, I skate into a restaurant parking lot, ride up to a bright yellow cement parking stop block, turn the board perpendicular to it, and railslide across its length. Smooth. I skate faster, then railslide across another block, gliding as if I were on ice. When I land it, my wheels make a satisfying smack. Under the endless blue sky, I'm off again, lost in the constant clatter of the wheels on the open stretch of street.

Some nights after eleven, when the sticky air cools, I ask to skate. It's past my curfew, but my parents let me stay out as long as I stick close to our house. In front of a square gray apartment complex, the street lamp becomes a spotlight. I push down on the tail of the McGill and pop an ollie. I pop some more, ollieing higher and higher, then drop down, my wheels bang-banging the pavement.

A woman from the apartment building yells, "Knock it off!"

But I haven't practiced kickflipping yet. I position my feet diagonally on the tail of the board, push down with my left foot, and kick my right foot out while pushing down on the board with my toe. I try to flip the board three hundred and sixty degrees, but it flies from beneath my feet into the air, and then lands on the ground, the skull facing up.

Again the woman from the apartment building yells, "Knock it off!"

I position my feet on the tail again, the way my cousin Ryan showed me to. Ryan is fifteen and taught me everything I know about skating; he showed me *Thrasher* magazine, skater clothes, and punk music, which is just as rad as skating. The Sex Pistols sing about the anti-Christ and anarchy. Dead Kennedys sing about Reagan's fascist ways and losing your freedom of speech. I know the lyrics. Most skaters do. But I don't know how to kickflip yet, so I position myself on the McGill again. I flip it three hundred and sixty degrees, but I don't land it.

The woman from the apartment building yells, "Knock it off! KNOCK IT OFF!"

Since she's getting pissed and the McGill landed right-side up—which means I'm getting closer to learning the trick—I head back inside.

All summer, whether I skate alone or with Ryan and his friends or some guys from my grade, I'm carried by the clatter of the wheels. Sometimes I skate around my neighborhood in the west end, a newer, quieter residential area. Sometimes I skate past the campus of the state university in the center of town, or ride to a friend's house in the east end, which is a bit "rougher" for a town of 25,000 people, partly because it's littered with bars.

On a hot day in August, I'm skating alone in the east end. A driver pulls up beside me in a rusted silver Honda Accord. The car is filled with a group of college men wearing white football jerseys with "Warriors" in purple lettering across the chest. A guy with short brown shaggy hair and a five o'clock shadow hangs his head out the window.

"Check out the skater girl," he calls out, his speech slurring. "Bitch."

From the passenger side, another one yells, "Nice hair, freak."

I try to steady my shaking legs, still skating.

The Warriors drive closer to me. One of them yells something about my clothes, but I don't fully hear him because I try to block out his voice, try to listen to the clatter of the wheels, and try to coax my arms and legs into doing what I know how to do: skate. Another man yells, "Dyke." I'm shaking and sweating everywhere. My neck. The small of my back. The backs of my knees.

The Warriors drive a few feet ahead of me. I can't skate faster than the Honda; I'm trapped. The same shaggy-haired guy leans out the window. He cocks his arm like a quarterback with the ball, but his hand is closed around whatever he's about to throw—I'm not sure and don't want to find out. I push off the pavement.

When the shaggy-haired guy releases whatever is in his hand, I freeze. When it's about to hit me, I see the white egg. It flies fast, punches me in the gut, bounces off me, and hits the street. The shell cracks. Yolk sprays my shin.

The Warriors drive off—maybe satisfied, or out of eggs. I breathe in and out, regaining the rhythm, regaining my balance, and begin skating again. The wheels clatter on, but my mind reels with slurred words, purple letters, a cocked arm, and the yolk-splattered street.

Trisha Speed Shaskan was born and raised in Winona, Minnesota, where she waterskied on the Mississippi River, played basketball, and skateboarded. She has written more than forty books for children and taught creative writing to children and teens. Trisha received a 2012 Minnesota State Artist's Initiative Grant. She won the 2009 McKnight Artist Fellowship for Writers, Loft Award in Children's Literature / Older Children. She lives in Minneapolis with her husband, Stephen Shaskan, who is a children's book author and illustrator.

DATING MAGIC

BY LAURIE EDWARDS

When I was eighteen and president of my house in college, I decided I'd make sure every single girl in the house had a date for the spring formal—not an easy feat at a school where the ratio of females to males was five to one. I started with my guy friends, making sure that anyone who didn't have a girlfriend was taking one of my housemates.

Then I went around the campus asking guys I barely knew if they'd let me fix them up with a date. Word spread, and soon guys I'd roped into taking dates dragged their dateless friends over to meet me. One by one, I paired them up with one of the girls in my house.

A week before the big day, I still needed escorts for three more girls. I'd run out of potential candidates, so when I saw this hot new guy in the cafeteria, a big neon sign flashed before my eyes: Potential Date Material.

I dashed over and, without even introducing myself, blurted out, "Do you have a date for the spring formal?"

He blinked and set down his fork. "Wow, if you're that desperate, I guess I could take you."

"No, no, I didn't mean for you to take me—that is, umm ...."

The way he was studying me with a teasing smile kept me tongue-tied. Up close he was even better looking. My face burning, I stumbled through an explanation about looking for dates for friends.

His one raised eyebrow indicated he didn't believe me. My stammering and blushing made my story less than convincing. Finally, with a quick "Never mind," I rushed off, hoping I'd never see him again.

The night of the formal, my chattering housemates primped and preened and paraded through the house showing off their glamour and glitz. I swirled before the mirror, wondering what it would be like to have someone else waiting for me downstairs. Spending that evening with my dependable date, a good friend for many years, was nice, but my imagination painted fairy-tale scenarios of me in the arms of a handsome stranger. One I'd be too embarrassed to face in real life.

The week after the formal, I was hurrying out of class and bumped into the handsome stranger from the cafeteria. Literally, that is. I slammed into his chest.

He reached out to prevent me from falling. "Throwing yourself at me again, eh? Oh, wait, I bet you're going to say you just did that for a friend."

"Not this time," I said. "But last time I really was looking for dates for my friends." I might have sounded a tad defensive.

He laughed. "I know. Guys in my dorm mentioned that you'd fixed them up. I probably wouldn't have gone anyway. I'm not really into going out with people I haven't met." That teasing smile returned. "But I suppose you could say we've met?"

Still trying to get my balance, I said the first thing that popped into my head. "I never introduced myself."

"Think we could remedy that?" he asked.

Staring into those clear hazel eyes made coherent thought impossible. My name? What was my name again? After an embarrassingly long silence, I managed to choke out, "Laurie."

He repeated my name in a deep bass voice that reverberated through my insides. Then he introduced himself and, to my total surprise, asked what I was doing that weekend.

If it had been left up to my constricted vocal chords, things might have ended there, but luckily he interpreted my gasping for air as a yes. And judging by the happy dance my heart did that Saturday night while I sat beside him at the movies, I had no doubt this might be the start of something magical.

Laurie Edwards ended up marrying that hot guy from the cafeteria, whose name is Richard. She still gets tongue-tied around people, but finds she's better at communicating on paper. She went on to become a freelance author, editor, and illustrator with a dozen books and more than two thousand articles in print. She is also the author of several adult and young adult novels written under pseudonyms.

BIG RED

BY JESSICA GUNDERSON

7:36. 7:37. 7:38.

I stared at the clock, hoping my death-stare would stop the progress of time until Sarah arrived. Finally I heard the spluttering chug of an engine making its way down the street. I knew the sound. It could only be Sarah.

Nausea was swimming in vicious, threatening laps around my stomach. I hadn't been nervous when I'd woken up this morning. The ACT was just a test, and I'd taken thousands of tests. In fact, I rather enjoyed taking tests. But suddenly, my heart triple-punched my rib cage, and a frightening, beady sweat-mustache sprouted above my upper lip. I caught a whiff of my hair. Bonfire, beer. Nausea threatened again.

Sarah met me at the kitchen door.

"You're late," I said.

"We're late," she said at the same time, and then she laughed.

I followed her to the driveway. She shouted something inaudible over the roar of the running engine. Sarah drove a 1949 cherry red Chevy truck. Whenever we paraded through town, everyone stared, although whether at Sarah or the truck, I don't know. She was the most exotic girl I'd ever known— long dark hair woven with gold, eyes of an indeterminate green-yellow-gray color, and full lips that broke often into a sparkling, wicked smile. She smoked long, skinny cigarettes that she flicked with her polished nails. Her entire being exuded experience and maturity, with a dash of mystery.

Sarah lived in a town about sixteen miles away. We'd met in junior high at a basketball game between our schools. I'd heard rumors that she was dating Kevin, the boy I liked at the time. My intention was to corner her in the bathroom and demand details, but when I approached her, she smiled at me and complimented my necklace. We'd been best friends ever since, writing each other letters, racking up phone bills, and spending the night at each other's houses. Now that we were juniors and Sarah had her truck, she drove to my town nearly every weekend. Wherever we went, guys stared, though I knew it wasn't at me. I felt awkward and mousy next to her, but a bit proud, too. I was her best friend. She'd chosen me.

The night before the test, we'd been cruising around when a car flashed its lights at us. We pulled over and Aaron Dillard, a senior and basketball player extraordinaire, ambled to Sarah's window. Every girl in my school wanted Aaron. He wasn't much to look at, in my opinion, but that didn't stop my heart from doing a little flip-flop when he leaned in the window, peered at me, and said, "Hi Jessica." He then turned to my friend. "You're Sarah, right?"

Although she wasn't from our town, Sarah'd heard of Aaron and his basketball prowess. Still, she just smiled and asked his name. He seemed a little taken aback but also somewhat intrigued.

Aaron invited us to follow him to a bonfire party out on a dead-end dirt road, a party spot dubbed "Big Red" due to the jocks who hung out there and the fact that our school color was red. I'd never been there before. I'd never been to any parties, actually. For one thing, I didn't drink. For another, my curfew was ungodly early—10 p.m. And for another, well, I'd never been invited.

We roared along the dirt road behind Aaron until we could see the glow of flames against the night sky. Sarah pulled over and we jumped out. She wore high, skinny-heeled boots but didn't even break her stride as she sauntered across the soft, weed-rutted road toward an open 24-pack of beer. She grabbed two, without asking and without hesitation, and cracked hers open, tossing the other to me.

Immediately she was surrounded by guys as if she were the only girl at the party, which she wasn't. There was me, of course, and a few others, mostly senior cheerleaders and volleyball players. I hung around the outskirts, pretending to drink my beer while watching Sarah flirt with each of the guys around her.

Someone threw more branches onto the fire and flames flared up, followed by a gush of black, thick smoke that soared directly into my nostrils. I coughed and stepped backward, bumping into a guy behind me.

"Sorry," I mumbled.

It was Adam Turnbull, the wide receiver on our football team. He blinked at me. "Jessica? What you doing here?" he said. Before I could respond, he looked down at my beer and laughed. "You know you gotta open the can before you can drink it."

Mortified, I looked down. Sure enough, I hadn't even opened the beer.

I held the can out to him. "I don't want it," I said. I was too embarrassed to tell him my curfew was 10 p.m., so I added, "I have ACTs in the morning."

I'd chosen the wrong thing to say and the wrong time to say it. The conversation around me had lulled, and my words rang strong and clear against the crackling of the fire.

"Nerd!" someone hollered, and the crowd broke into demonic laughter. Their faces bobbed in the firelight, glowing orbs split by black grimaces.

Sarah moved toward me. "Let's go," she said. She tossed her beer can into the fire, and it landed with a sloshy, heavy thud. I realized she hadn't been drinking hers, either.

"He asked for my phone number," Sarah told me as we pulled away from the party. "But I didn't give it to him."

"Aaron did? Why on earth not?"

She shrugged. "It'll keep him guessing."

When she pulled into my driveway, I saw my mom silhouetted in the window, looking out. I glanced at my watch. It was 10:02.

I jumped from the truck, and Sarah called out the window, "I'll pick you up at 7:30!"

* * *

It was now 7:51. As we rumbled down the street to the school, Sarah pulled a cigarette from her pack. "Gawd. I need a cigarette before this test."

"We don't have time!" I said. "And besides, your cigarettes give me a headache."

She lit it anyway and veered left, away from the school. By the time we pulled into the parking lot, it was 7:59. My head was pounding and my throat tight. I ran toward the school as fast as my non-athletic body would carry me, and Sarah breezed past, laughing.

We plunged through the door of the assembly room at 8:01. The test administrator was speaking, and he stopped abruptly as we entered. He was scary-looking—tall and bone-thin, shoulders like meat hooks, and fat hands that dangled sausage-like fingers. "You are late!" he thundered. I crouched toward the nearest open desk, but Sarah tossed her hair, grinning as she scanned the room for a place to sit and waving at a few kids from her school.

The test began, but I couldn't focus. My head felt split in

two. I needed a drink of water. My pencil was dull. The scary test administrator was pacing. My hair smelled.

Focus, I told myself. Focus.

I glanced at Sarah. She clutched her pencil so tightly her knuckles were white. With her other hand she pulled at her hair, something she only did on the rare occasion she was nervous.

I stared at the words on the page. The English section. I should be good at this part. I needed to relax.

I looked up again. The assembly room was the brightest room in the building, with wide windows at the front and a billion fluorescent lights overhead. Around the top perimeter of the room hung photographs of graduating classes from years past. As I gazed blankly, I realized I was staring at the Class of 1936. My grandmother's class. Her face smiled out at me among the stern-faced boys around her. She'd been the only girl to graduate that year.

I followed the pictures until I found the Class of 1964. My mother's class. She smiled out at me, too.

It hit me then that I would be the third generation of women in my family to graduate from this school. And, like my mother, I would go on to college. Yes, I strived to be like Sarah: popular, confident, and beautiful. But I realized I also wanted my grandmother's strength and intelligence, my mother's drive and passion. I didn't need to prove myself at parties with jocks and beer. I just needed to have faith that I could be as strong and beautiful as the other women in my life.

I gripped my pencil and began.

Jessica Gunderson grew up in North Dakota and currently lives in Madison, Wisconsin, across the street from a high school. She admits that she sometimes eavesdrops on the students who pass by. She'll never use their stories in her writing—she promises! She is the author of numerous books for young readers, all written in her very messy office.

CONFESSIONS OF A
PRETEND BOYFRIEND

BY AARON BROWN

A pudgy, nearsighted freshman active in speech, drama, and
the Future Farmers of America generally doesn't find himself
invited to senior prom. Particularly if he lives fifteen miles away
from the school out in a swampy section of forgotten land, far
from where the other kids grew up together. Nevertheless, I
got an early taste of prom my freshman year, at the invitation
of a beautiful blond high school senior who had played my
girlfriend in the school play that winter. She was a very good
actress, as far as I could tell.

Tall, buxom with a cascading laugh and a working
awareness of science fiction movies, she was a prom date cast
from the imagination of a rural nerd, rendered real by my
unremitting good luck. What could possibly go wrong with a
situation as glorious as this one? Well, for one, we were just
friends. She had a boyfriend who was in the Army and was

always away doing Army Things, which made him the perfect boyfriend for her to have as far as I was concerned. On prom day, I was ready for the magic. Who knows, maybe I'd even tell her how I really felt, even though it might (sigh) jeopardize our friendship.

Then the call came. Army Boyfriend had come home to surprise her for her senior prom. I had only seen Army Boyfriend in photographs and, though he had graduated from my small school just the year before, I would never have heard of him were it not for his inconvenient attachment to my prom date. Even in the pictures he looked theoretical. My friend was perpetually a year younger than she was now; not as beautiful and poised. This was not reality.

But Army Boyfriend was real, and on the day of prom she called to inform me that he had returned from Fort FistPunch, but don't worry! He's cool with us still going together. Only, he'll be there too. Oh, yeah, he's an Army Ranger now. She didn't say it, but I knew that meant that not only could he beat me up, but he could break my neck in a way that would make it look like a heart attack.

"That's ... fine," I said. What was I going to say? I had the tux. It matched her dress.

We met in the lobby of the ballroom. His piercing sniper eyes could read the washing instructions on the tag of my shirt. His handshake was an audition for a play about construction equipment. He wasn't threatened by me. No, far worse. He was annoyed.

She went through the grand march twice, once with me and once with the Army Ranger, whose crisp dress greens did not match her gown. There were two sets of pictures. One with me, and one with the Army Ranger. I got one dance with her that night, which was the same number of dances I got with her best friend and the French teacher, both of which were blatant mercy dances.

At one point the Army Ranger and my friend were sitting next to each other across the table from me playing a cute little couple's game of guessing what was in the guy's wallet. "I give up, what is it?" she asked about a slip of paper.

"It's the receipt for my gun," he said.

"Ha! (pause) Ha! Ha!" I added. "I am having a very good time!"

There were parties afterward, but as the conversation halted for several blaring dance hits, it was silently understood that I would not be attending. There would be pie at the restaurant where my friend and I had our first date that, in retrospect, probably wasn't a date.

I rode home in the backseat of his car.

As I walked on the wet, muddy driveway back up to my house, the amorous frogs were all too vocal in explaining that their night had gone much better than mine. I wasn't a boyfriend. I had just played one on stage. Some drama doesn't come with a script.

Aaron Brown won the Weekly Reader National Invention Contest in second grade. Having peaked early, he retired to write his memoirs in the mighty pine forest of northern Minnesota. He writes stuff for things in places you find on the Internet, most notably his blog MinnesotaBrown.com.

SOLO

BY ESTHER PORTER

Minutes before the last concert of our tenth-grade year, my choir friends and I waited on the bleachers near the stage in our school's gymnasium. They sat on one end, giddy to have completed finals, and I sat alone on the other, trying to breathe slowly. I stared at my shoes, the horrible strappy high heels that dug into my ankles. My stomach was in knots. Every time I looked up, the audience grew.

Our choir director had given me the solo for "The Look of Love." She told me to "stay relaxed" and sing like Dusty Springfield. When I told her I'd never heard of Dusty Springfield, she played me a recording from the 1960s. I was surprised to hear a woman's voice that sounded both smooth and gravelly, relaxed yet precise. Careful with every note. Dusty Springfield was a woman from another time, and the strength of her voice was beyond me. As I waited on the bleachers, I thought back to that recording. The idea of keeping my cool in front of hundreds of people made me dizzy.

My friends weren't helping the situation either. They must have thought I was on a high horse because of the solo, sitting so far away from them. They took turns glaring in my direction.

I had to get out of there. Without saying a word, I jumped off the bleachers and pushed through the heavy doors to a small hallway behind the gymnasium. When the door slammed shut, I sat down with my back against the wall. The sudden silence made the air feel empty, and my nerves began to calm. I breathed into my stomach the way we were told to in choir practice. I loved singing because it forced me to breathe in a way that calmed me. It helped me regulate myself from the inside so I could relax into the music. However stressed I was, singing with a choir felt like therapy. But now I had to figure out how to sing alone and go out there solo without the protection of a choir.

I looked up at a bulletin board on the wall and saw a map of the school. It was a bird's-eye view. I closed my eyes and imagined floating up, beyond the hallway and the gymnasium, beyond all the people piling in, even beyond the school, until I was floating above the building. From this view, I saw that everything in the school—the hallways, the gymnasium—could be seen as one thing.

I opened my eyes. The courage to sing alone wasn't something I had to find in the gymnasium somewhere. I had practiced enough that I carried the song inside of myself.

I stood up and opened the heavy doors. A hundred faces turned to me, and I froze. I paid attention to the air at my back, still in the hallway. I was in both places at once, but I closed my eyes and remembered the view from far away.

As my choir friends took their places, I walked to the front of the stage. I looked into the audience and saw people who, after that night's concert, I wouldn't see for the whole summer. I suddenly felt lonely. By losing my fear, it seemed I had lost something else. It was as if the concert no longer mattered. I decided, rather than losing my fear, I would let it in, but wouldn't let it control me. My stomach fluttered and my heart lifted. I opened my eyes, took a deep breath, and sang my own version of Dusty's song.

Esther Porter grew up in North Dakota, where she and her best friend had enough small animals to open a zoo. She is the author of a number of science-y books including What's Sprouting in My Trash? A Book about Composting *and* Sun Power: A Book about Renewable Energy. *Her only animals now are Chopstick the angry cat, Georgie the confused cat, and Samantha Turkey Porter the slobbery pup.*

SINGING ALONG

BY KARA BALCERZAK

When I was sixteen years old, I spent most of my energy trying
to hide. I hid behind books and behind baggy clothes, behind
silence, behind the assumption that most people in my classes
or on the swim team or in my school at large didn't know who
I was. And if they did know, they didn't care.

Alma, on the other hand, was the most outgoing person
I'd ever met. Everybody knew her. People at parties gathered
around just to hear her tell a ten-minute joke about the color
pink. And the joke wasn't even funny, but people laughed
anyway. She had that spark.

My friendship with Alma was unlikely. The first time I
remember talking to Alma was at a swim meet as we stood on
the pool deck, chlorine thick in the air, the sounds of splashing
and whistles behind us.

"Is there any band you'd pay a hundred dollars to go see?"
she asked.

"I'd probably pay that to see Live."

"Ooh, Live." She paused, her towel in one hand. "Yeah, I'd pay that to see Live."

From there, Alma and I quickly became friends. We talked about Live constantly. On the bus to swim meets, we synched up our Discman CD players and listened to the albums simultaneously, singing along.

Alma and I spent entire days in front of MTV, VHS tapes poised to record the moment a Live video began. At a music store in Alexandria, we got bootleg CDs of concert recordings and incorporated the lead singer's offhand comments in between songs into our conversations in the halls at school. "It's a York, Pennsylvania, thing," we'd say, a reference to the band's hometown.

We fed each other's obsession. We joined an email fan club and shared news with other fans. We knew the name of the high school where the band members had met (William Penn Senior High) and the name of the lead singer's pet turtle (Murti). We analyzed Live's lyrics in a way that would have made our English teachers proud, trading interpretations about lead singer and songwriter Ed Kowalczyk's recurring references to water, his questioning of religious dogma, and his references to love—not romantic love, but a deep kind of love Ed seemed to feel for the world. In Ed's lyrics I saw hints at answers to questions I was just starting to ask.

* * *

A year after our obsession began, Live came to the 9:30 Club in Washington, D.C., just twenty miles from where we lived in the Virginia suburbs. We knew we had to go. The band usually played large arenas, so tickets for the small venue went fast. They sold them only at the club, and even though we got there just hours after they went on sale, they sold out before we reached the front of the line. For weeks afterward we tried to win them on the radio. We ditched the cafeteria and ate lunch every day in the journalism office, where there was a radio and phone. Whenever they played a Live song, you had to be caller nine to win. We were caller number five, seven, ten, two, and even one, but never magic number nine.

Finally, the day of the show arrived. We still didn't have tickets, but we decided to head to the club anyway. I knew my parents wouldn't approve, so I left the house before they got home from work, picked up Alma, and drove to the closest mall that had a subway stop. We took the subway into the city and only then called my parents from a pay phone with a made-up story about how Alma's college-aged brother had gotten tickets from a friend and would drive us to the show, protect us from drunks, and hold our hands when we crossed busy streets.

In reality, we were two sixteen-year-old girls on our own. We spent the next four hours on the cracked sidewalk outside the club, asking everyone who walked by if they had an extra ticket. We quickly got one at face value off a group of teenagers waiting in line and almost couldn't believe our luck. But then hours passed, and no one else had an extra ticket. We talked about what to do with our single shared ticket. We wondered whether we could take turns going in and laid claims on which songs we each wanted to be inside to hear. But then finally, just an hour before the doors were going to open, a scalper showed up and agreed to sell us a second ticket at double its face value. He led me down an alley to take my forty-five bucks. I imagined a swarm of cops was watching us, just waiting for me to pull out my cash before they threw handcuffs on my wrists. Or maybe the scalper was planning to grab my money and run. But these fears didn't stop me; Live was within my grasp. I followed the guy down the street, handed him my cash, and grabbed the ticket from his outstretched hand. I ran back to Alma, shaking with the realization that it was really happening. We were going to see Live.

We spent the next two hours trembling in disbelief. Despite having claimed spots just feet from the stage, I barely registered the opening act. When Live finally took the stage, I screamed incoherently through the entire first song, trying to make sense of how these people whose videos and interviews I'd watched over and over for the last year could be in my physical presence, playing the songs that had come to mean so much to me. Their new album had been out for barely a week, but we didn't miss a word as we sang along. Occasionally I noticed the people around us, mostly people in their twenties who were standing around with their hands jammed into their pockets, shouting conversations into each other's ears or casually leaving in the middle of songs to go to the bathroom or buy drinks. But then I'd look over at Alma and see her dancing, or see her eyes closed with emotion as she sang and the guitars swelled around us, and I felt so lucky to be sharing this night with someone else who knew exactly how much it meant.

After the show—which naturally was far too short—we took the subway back to the mall parking garage where we'd left my car. It was almost midnight. The mall—and therefore the garage—had closed hours earlier, and a narrow plastic arm blocked the exit, its control booth locked and empty. I sat behind the wheel. I turned off the car. We stared at the arm, wondering if we were going to have to spend the night there. Finally Alma got out and pushed against the arm. It jostled a little, and she pushed harder until it rose a few feet, just high enough that the car could slip under.

We escaped the mall and sped down Interstate 395 through the dark night. The energy of the music vibrated through the car. It was after midnight, but I was wide awake. Outside, a handful of cars sped along the highway. It felt like all of them were with us, coming from the concert. It felt like all of us could be heading anywhere.

Kara Garbe Balcerzak grew up in Springfield, Virginia, a suburb of Washington, D.C. Most of her writing is about living in a mud house in Burkina Faso, where she was a Peace Corps volunteer after college. Kara has seen Live in concert more than a dozen times since 1997, most recently in 2013. She and Alma are still good friends.

HARD TO SWALLOW

BY JENNA SCARBROUGH

As I sat cross-legged on my bed four months ago, I ran my hand down my neck, rubbing my skin. I was halfway through my freshman year in college. So far, it had been uneventful. My hand stopped when I felt a lump on my throat, the size of half a ping-pong ball, protruding slightly to the right of the center and directly under my Adam's apple. My pulse raced as I considered one possible explanation.

***

I plugged my phone into the car adapter to play some music through the speakers as my mom drove me to yet another appointment. I scrolled past Vampire Weekend, The National, and Lucius before finally selecting a song. I picked "Casimir Pulaski Day" by Sufjan Stevens, a mellow song about the death of a girl with cancer. If I had to suffer through another doctor appointment, I might as well enjoy being morbid.

"How long do you think this will last?" I asked my mom, who had been silent for the first few minutes of the ride across town.

Her eyes stayed glued to the road. "An hour or so. Why? Do you have plans?"

I shrugged but said nothing. My social life didn't really involve plans. My friends enjoyed the kind of things most nineteen-year-olds do: sitting around, eating Ben & Jerry's, and talking. This was our standard hangout activity, but somehow it never got old. Our trio—my friend, my roommate, and I— always felt incomplete when one of us was missing, and lately I had been the one responsible for the absences. I longed for the comfort of my dorm room instead of the frigid air and to laugh along with my friends instead of spending time on an examining table.

"Thyroid cancer is the most treatable kind of cancer," my endocrinologist, Dr. Babu, told my mom and me. The tall Indian woman stooped over me as I sat in my thin hospital gown on the thin sheet of white examining paper. She pulled on a pair of rubber gloves and lightly pressed against the lump in my throat. "Does this hurt?" I shook my head. She continued, "The chances of it being cancerous are slim. Right now you're standing at about ten percent. If we decide you're at risk, however, we'll probably recommend you have surgery and just remove part of the thyroid."

Dr. Babu caught the expression on my face. "Like I said, chances are it's not cancerous. If we do the surgery, you'd have to take supplementary vitamins to replace the hormones it can no longer make. But you wouldn't need any radiation or chemotherapy. Now, have you experienced any unexpected weight gain? Difficulty swallowing or breathing?"

"No," I said. "It's really only this lump. That's my only symptom."

I thought back to my first visit to the doctor over Christmas break. The doctor had asked me similar questions to what Dr. Babu was aking in order to see if the lump was a concern. They had then sent me to have an ultrasound the next day. Through this test, the endocrinologists detected two nodules in my throat—one was the lump I had felt, which was just over a centimeter in diameter. The other was smaller and unnoticeable by touch, but was just big enough to be concerning.

Dr. Babu cleared her throat. "Your ultrasound results were inconclusive, so I'm going to send you to the lab to have some blood drawn. We just want to make sure your thyroid is working correctly, so we know for sure that the lump isn't cancerous."

A week after the blood extraction, my lab results came back. All hormones in my body were at normal levels. The doctors asked to perform another test—a biopsy. The procedure would require eight extractions—four from each nodule—of tissue from my thyroid. Eight more needles puncturing my flesh was not my idea of fun, but I wanted to get to the bottom of this.

I hoped the biopsy would be the last test they would perform. I realized by now that something had to be wrong, or they would have told me long ago what the problem was. I couldn't imagine what it would be like to have cancer. The doctors kept trying to make it sound like thyroid cancer wouldn't be a big deal, but I knew the truth: Receiving this news would require me to face many of my fears, such as receiving needles in my arms for blood tests. I might not lose my hair or anything, but I had never had surgery before, or even broken a bone, so the idea of being sick really scared me. Even if the operation was a complete success, I'd have to take pills for the rest of my life. I'd always had a hard time swallowing pills, and I hated the idea of having to take one every day until I die.

I tried to suppress my paranoia during each of these tests. Thoughts like these were the last thing that needed to be on my mind.

* * *

I spent the day after the biopsy playing phone tag with the clinic. I went to my classes anyway, trying to focus. Toward the end of my last class, while we watched a German film, I looked down at my phone and saw the screen was lit: one missed call. My heart pounded. As soon as Professor Clark dismissed class, I sprinted down the stairs and redialed the number. The receptionist transferred my call to the endocrinologist, and standby jazz began playing in my ear. Finally I heard a response on the other end.

Dr. Babu's strong accent was difficult to understand over the phone. "We have gotten the lab results back," she said, "and it seems that the samples we've extracted look suspicious. We can't tell for sure right now, but the odds of it being cancerous are now up to seventy or eighty percent."

That word: cancer.

"So what's next?" I tried to keep my voice steady.

"The next step is surgery," she said. "That will remove potentially all of the suspicious cells. We are still unsure whether they are cancerous, but we don't want to risk it. I would suggest getting it done sometime in the next month or two, but you probably don't want to wait any longer than that."

I thanked her and hung up, trying to absorb the news. Everything about having cancer seemed daunting to me: missing classes to have a knife in my throat, gulping down pills every morning, and receiving Facebook messages from relatives telling me they are praying for me.

When I got back to my dorm, my roommate and two other friends were laughing and joking. I waited for a lull in their conversation before interjecting with my news.

"I just got off the phone with the doctor," I told them calmly. "They said it's likely I have thyroid cancer. So I guess I'll have to get surgery, but that'll take care of it. Nothing to really worry about, I think. That's what the doctors told me, anyway."

That was it. Just a few simple sentences to explain the spreading of thousands of diseased cells inside my body, to explain the plummet my heart had just taken. I was surprised by how steady my voice had sounded, even to me.

"That sucks," one of them said.

Standing there, I realized they wouldn't understand what this felt like. The more I thought about it, the more I realized that if they'd asked me how I was, I would have just lied. I would've pretended to be strong, and they would've probably brushed it off anyway, thinking I was telling the truth. I realized none of my friends would understand. They knew the facts; they couldn't know the feelings.

Later, alone in my room, I grabbed my phone and sent my mom a request to FaceTime. Her face appeared on the small screen.

"Have the doctors contacted you yet?" I asked her.

She shook her head. "No, they haven't. I've been at work all day." Her voice sounded thin and tired. "Why? What's the news?"

I told her everything and watched her expression shift as I continued explaining what little information I had obtained from the doctors. I could see her eyes cloud with tears and her face flush.

"But they said they could treat all of it if they just did the operation," I said, as if it was my job to reassure her, not the other way around.

"It's going to be okay. Just hang in there." Her strained voice did not convince me. "Do you want me to drive up to school? I can be there in three hours."

I shook my head.

"I'm going to call the doctors and see if I can get more details," she said. "I love you."

I hung up the phone and looked out the window, not really focusing on anything outside. I played our conversation over again in my head, analyzing her reaction to the news. Moms are supposed to know how to fix everything. My mother's uncertainty made me feel even more uneasy, as if the doctors were wrong and it was more serious than a simple procedure. It's treatable, it's treatable, it's treatable, I reminded myself over and over. I could get through this. I just needed a bit of courage.

Jenna Scarbrough attends college in Minnesota and sometimes admits to living in South Dakota. She can neither confirm nor deny allegations that she and her twin sister switched places on occasion in high school. She can confirm an unsuccessful attempt prior to her recent surgery.

BEST FRIENDS

BY RACHAEL HANEL

Through fifth and sixth grades, Jenni Snyder and I shared a "best friends" necklace. On the necklace's chain hung a cheap silver-colored heart inscribed with the words "best friends." A zigzag line broke the necklace in two, and Jenni and I each wore one half.

One day toward the end of sixth grade, while I was riding the bus home, my hand went to my neck to play with the necklace as I always did. But the necklace was not there. Frantic, I looked around the dirty floor. It could have been anywhere—near my desk at school, on the playground, in the bathroom. It was lost.

The next day, another friend of mine said, "You know what they say, don't you?"

I didn't.

"If you lose a best friends necklace, the friendship is lost, too."

* * *

It wasn't true, or so I thought, because Jenni and I made it through that summer together. At her house we listened to Whitney Houston, played basketball on her small driveway court, and gossiped about boys. I thought it would always be that way.

As fall turned into winter during seventh grade, Jenni decided she wanted to be popular. There was no proclamation, but I could see the way she eyed the lunch table where the alpha girls sat. I'd see her in the hallways or classrooms laughing at their jokes and finding ways to talk to them.

I wasn't invited along in Jenni's quest. It wasn't like she said, "Let's be popular together!" She must not have seen even a glimmer of potential in me. My parents were blue collar; they worked for themselves. Dad was a gravedigger, and he and Mom also mowed cemeteries. But this wasn't odd; most families in this small Minnesota town were working class.

My parents earned a decent living. We always had plenty of food on the table, and Dad and Mom had even bought a used Cadillac. Up until I was in first grade, we lived in a double-wide trailer house, but then Dad put a basement underneath so it seemed more like a "real" house. My clothes were clean and neat.

But they weren't the right clothes, at least by popular standards. My jeans didn't have brand-name triangle patches on back pockets. My sweatshirts didn't have bright, big logos. At the time, a pair of jeans or a sweatshirt like that could easily cost forty dollars. Mom and Dad, both raised by farmer parents who struggled through the Great Depression, would've never considered spending that kind of money on clothes. Jenni's parents had more money than mine did. Her dad ran a business, and her mom was a nurse. She was the baby of the family and spoiled. If she wanted name-brand clothes, she got them.

Jenni's break from me was so clean and fast that it left me spinning. One day in the lunchroom, I watched her glide past our table, lunch tray in hand, eyes not daring to glance at me, and plop herself down at a table with the popular girls—Sarah, Jess, and Tiffany. The parents of these girls had money—they were white-collar professionals who worked in insurance, business, and education. These girls had the right clothes and the attention of the popular boys.

Jenni gave me no transitional period, no warning. I saw two options from there. I could either let it destroy me, or I could pick myself up and move on. I chose the latter. Once I stopped feeling sorry for myself, I took a close look around. I saw other girls who also had been rejected. We were the castoffs, the rejects. I didn't know these girls well at first, but we would bond over our shared experiences, our common backgrounds of rural blue-collar stock, and our clothes that didn't have labels.

* * *

I never spoke to Jenni again through junior high and high school. Our class in my smallish town was about 170 students; the entire high school had 600 students. This meant I saw Jenni often—in classes, at lunch, in marching band. But it's surprisingly easy to avoid eye contact when you want to.

Jenni remained friends with that same seventh-grade lunchroom group through high school. I remained friends with the castoff group. I was able to move seamlessly among different social circles—I was a little bit athlete, a little bit musician, a little bit drama nerd, and a lot academic. One circle I kept my distance from, though, was Jenni's circle. I was wary of them and forever associated "popular" with "fickle." These were girls who might be my friends one day and not the next.

When my father died unexpectedly the summer between my freshman and sophomore years, several friends reached out to me. Jenni, once my best friend, didn't call. Instead she sent a generic card co-signed with another classmate, one of the lunchroom girls whom I barely knew and didn't care to know. It was a nice sympathy card with its canned pleasantries, but it had just their signatures—no additional handwritten sentiments. It was like a card you'd send to a business associate.

I saw Jenni at our ten-year high school reunion. I learned she had become a successful dentist; I was not surprised. I saw firsthand the way she set a goal for herself and went after it with gusto. But I was surprised by the hurt that surfaced when I saw her, as if seventh grade had been just the year before, not fifteen years in the past. I had my own successes at that point—a job I loved, a husband I loved, and opportunities like running and cycling that made me more confident than I ever had been in junior high. The woman I had become was far different than the girl left bruised by a broken friendship. Talking to Jenni that night would bring back that sad girl, and I didn't want to see her again. I stayed on the other side of the room. It still was surprisingly easy to avoid eye contact, even in a small room, when you really wanted to.

* * *

Twenty years after high school, twenty-five years after we had last talked, Jenni and I finally spoke. It was another reunion, and when I saw Jenni, again I instinctively turned the other way. Old habits die hard.

I had just published a memoir about my childhood and teenage years growing up as the daughter of a gravedigger. One moment found me alone, and I looked at the empty drink in my hand and turned to get another. I felt a tap at my elbow. I spun around to see Jenni.

"Hi, Rachael!"

"Jenni—hi!"

Jenni hadn't changed much. She was still the petite girl with dark hair and infectious laugh that I had spent so much time with.

She wanted to talk about my book.

"I was reading through it, and there was my name!" she said. I had mentioned her as one of the friends who played with me in the cemetery; one of the few friends who did so.

She had me sign her book, on the page where she appears. She thanked me, and we chatted about jobs and families.

Then: "I just have to say something to you," she said. "I feel so bad that I never reached out. We were such good, good friends, and I feel terrible that I never said anything to you. That was just rotten. What a terrible friend I was."

I didn't know what to say. I hadn't expected this at all. I'm not sure anyone had ever apologized to me in person before. "We were so young," I said. "We were just learning our way in the world. No one can fault us for the things we did or didn't do back then."

She smiled and looked a little lighter; apologies have that effect.

We parted again.

Someone snapped our picture that night. I look at it often. I'm nearly forty years old and spent just two years with this girl, five percent of my life. Why does that five percent still loom so large? Jenni represents when life was good. My dad was alive. Jenni and I were just kids with no worries or obligations. Jenni's breakup with me was the first bad thing that had happened to me. At age thirteen, it was my entry into an adult world that could be fractious, dark, and sad. It was my first breakup but wouldn't be my last. If it hadn't been Jenni, it would have been someone else.

Rachael Hanel was born in Minnesota, where she still resides. She's the author of We'll Be the Last Ones to Let You Down: Memoir of a Gravedigger's Daughter, *and you're likely to find her roaming around cemeteries.*

SMILING JOE

BY JOSEPH BRUCHAC

Smiling Joe. It was my junior year when I first earned that nickname. I hadn't yet "gotten my growth," as we used to say. I had not yet added on the five inches in height and thirty pounds or so in weight that would transform me from geek to jock in one head-spinning twelve-month span. I wasn't all that popular then. I was a hick kid from the country with an irritatingly large vocabulary, a penchant for poetry, and, to be honest, an underlying shyness.

One particular spring day, during the lunch hour break when we were allowed to leave the school, I had trailed a bunch of other boys two blocks down Lake Avenue to Lee's Store. Lee's was a popular hangout, not just for the candy and soda and other snacks we could buy there, but also for Mr. Goodwin, a storeowner who both tolerated and liked teenagers and had a great sense of humor. His wisecracks were wry and amusing, but never hurtful. He had named the little general store for his son.

I'm not sure what I was smiling about, nervously in all likelihood, as I sat on the steps of the store that day. But a bigger kid in my class named Red, who had a reputation as a bully, took note of my smile and that it might be construed as being aimed in his general direction. He stepped up to me.

"What are you smiling at?"

I said the first thing that came into my head. The wrong thing, of course. "Nothing."

"You sayin' I'm nothing, you little creep?"

I realized right away what was happening. What should have occurred next was either that I would back down and be shown up as a yellowbellied coward or that I would get the crap knocked out of me. For some reason that just made my grin get bigger. I stood up and let my vocabulary take over.

"No, quite the contrary, my good fellow. I am relatively sure that you are something. Though whether it is Neanderthal or Picanthropoid is somewhat beyond my powers of deduction."

It was almost a knockout punch. Or at least the equivalent of a jab. It made Red step back for a moment and shake his head while he tried to decipher what had just been said.

But then, recovering from my verbal assault, he grabbed my wrist and tried to twist it. Without success. Although I'd never been in a fight before—if that was what was happening—I was stronger than I looked. The baggy clothes my beloved grandmother dressed me in disguised the fact that even at 150 pounds and 5-foot-9 I wasn't soft. My favorite pastime back then was to roam the woods behind our house and climb to the top of the tallest trees I could find.

I looked at Red, and he looked at me. Then he grabbed my arm with two hands. Curious about what his plan was, I let him take it. He lifted my arm and slammed it as hard as he could down onto his raised knee. Which did produce a result.

"Ow, ow, ow!"

And as I stood there looking down at Red rolling around on the ground and holding onto his bruised knee, I have to admit I felt a little sorry for him.

But I was still smiling.

***

As I was that summer when I launched myself off the high board at the Victoria Pool in a perfect swan dive. Hoping to impress Susie Boyle, the blond optometrist's daughter on whom I had an unrequited crush. Who didn't even notice either my attempt at scoring a perfect 10 or my incarnadined and somewhat flatter face as I came up after hitting the concrete bottom.

"Man, oh man! You are a mess and you broke off your front tooth," Ralph the lifeguard gasped as I swam to the edge and looked up at him where he was standing at the top of the ladder.

"It's okay," I said with a smile. "At least I didn't lose one of my canine teeth."

"Are you crazy?" was his reply.

And, uh-huh, I just smiled at him through my bloody drool.

* * *

I ended up with a temporary cap on that tooth, courtesy of Dr. Bennett, our far-from-pain-free family dentist. A silver cap, to be precise. Only slightly less visible than a headlight in the middle of my mouth. At the request of the professional photographer who snapped my yearbook picture, my smile was with closed lips.

But the grin that was on my face during every wrestling match of my senior year, exposed that highly artificial addition to my dentition. So much so that when I went to Cornell (with a more natural ivory-colored cap like the one I wear to this day) I was approached by a student who was in my English Comp class and had graduated from Linton, one of the schools we wrestled against during my last high school year. The year a news piece in the *Saratogian* referred to me as "Smiling Joe Bruchac, the Western Conference tournament winner."

My fellow college frosh was, it turned out, astounded that I was one of the two best students in that comp class. "Man," the Linton guy said (and forgive what follows, as I faithfully report it in the words he used at the time), "with that stupid grin of yours we all thought you were retarded."

***

I suppose it may be because of that smile that there's been more than one time in my life when I've been judged as clueless, naïve, or even insincere. And I've heard this remark: "One of these days, Bruchac, you'll learn that there's nothing to smile about."

There's an old Iroquois story I have loved since I first heard it more than five decades ago. It's the story of the Boy Who Defeated All His Enemies Through Laughter. One after another he faces terrible creatures that try to kill him. For example, when he goes to a deep spring where a monster that has been eating people lives, the creature rises up and bites off both of the boy's legs. In response the boy just laughs. And as he laughs, his legs grow back. Then, still laughing, he pulls that terrible being out of the water and beats it to death with a club.

***

A Mohawk elder and friend Tom Porter (whose Indian name Sakokwenionkwas means "The One Who Wins") once explained it to me this way: We human beings have the ability to change our minds. We can, quite literally, change the way we are thinking. We may find ourselves in what is sometimes called the Twisted Mind. That is when we are thinking and acting selfishly, angrily, or deep in self-pity and complaining that life is unfair.

Or we may choose to think and behave otherwise, put ourselves into the Good Mind. Then we realize that life is just life. We return to kindness and generosity, to patience—with others and with ourselves. We can laugh again—and smile.

Joseph Bruchac lives in the Adirondack Mountain foothills town of Greenfield Center, New York, in the same house where his maternal grandparents raised him. Much of his writing draws on that land and his Abenaki ancestry. He has been a storyteller-in-residence for Native American organizations and schools throughout the continent, including the Institute of Alaska Native Arts and the Onondaga Nation School.

THE LATTER DAYS OF JEAN

BY REBECCA STANBOROUGH

I came out here to the backyard shed, with the shutters and doors and cottony pink insulation, to write this down before time takes any of the memory of what happened to us because of Granny Jean Gunter.

When I was sixteen, my family split apart and I came here to the Genesis Community House, a kind of shelter for artsy teenagers who needed a place to belong. Little by little I've felt myself stealing down into the soil of the place, but I didn't really take hold until we got our Granny Jean, and her life depended almost entirely on us.

She was not my blood Granny. I was friends with her daughters, Laura and Beth—but the little kids here called her Granny Jean, so it seemed natural that I should, too, especially after sickness etched lines in her and slowed her pace.

I remember going to dinner at the Gunters' on Sunday afternoons.

"Hello, hello, hello!" Jean would call. There was always a waif or two at the table, along with pretty girls, fancy from church, jingling their car keys. And there was this dessert called "the orange stuff" that Jean made out of Jell-O and whipped cream and I don't know what all. There never was a bit of it left over afterward.

As the biscuits went around, Jack (Jean's husband) would ask, "Well, what's going on over to your house?" You could tell them whatever was going on, even if it didn't seem right for the table, because that's the way they were. Ordinary but special, like the hummingbirds out in Jack's garden, all enchanted-looking, and with your slightest twitch, gone into the hibiscus.

I remember one time, Jack and Jean performed at the Christmas gala. Everybody was dressed up in sequins, and here came Jack and Jean onto the stage, ukuleles and overalls, gray hair sticking out of straw hats. They sang this song to the tune of "Just a Closer Walk with Thee":

Just a bowl of butterbeans.
Pass the cornbread, if you please.
I don't want no turnip greens,
just a bowl, a bowl of butterbeans.

Their real talent was throwing parties. Slumber parties, Christmas parties, No Reason parties. One time, they fixed this great big banana split that spread the whole way down three picnic tables, end to end. That was about the time Jean first got sick. Colon cancer. But she didn't give in, and after a while, she got better. We didn't think anything else about it until six months ago, when she started feeling bad again.

I don't like to admit it, but I was afraid. Liver cancer, they said. But Kathleen, my second mother, said Jean's latter days would be better than her former, like Job's. I believed her.

You'd think Jean would have gone home and made some peace for herself, but she didn't. She started coming over to our loud house, with the fifteen of us and our neighbors traipsing in and out. At first it was just dinner. Jack helped her onto a kitchen stool and she'd cut up chickens and talk all afternoon. Then he'd help her back into the Oldsmobile, and they'd be gone until next time.

One day after they'd gone, Kat looked up from chopping onions and said, "Jean is my mother, in the spirit. I feel it."

So when the doctors said there was nothing else they could do, Granny Jean moved in. We fixed her a bed in the living room.

I came in from school one day, and Jean said, "Aren't I beautiful? Little Rachel here has fixed up my hair!" She had two-dozen blue barrettes sticking up all over her head in every direction. Another time, Janet was giving Jean a bath when she realized there was no soap. She had to go clear to the other end of the house to get some. So Granny Jean waited. And waited.

"Finally," she said, "I got cold! So I pushed down the drain lever with my toe and let the water run out, and I put a bathmat over me in case a man walked in. Then I heard someone, so I yelled 'Help!' Rachel came in, and I said, 'Rachel, go get Janet.' She said, 'I can't, Granny Jean. Janet's gone to the bank!'" It was a long time before Jean took another bath.

Mostly she lay on the scratchy sofa bed, reading *Southern Living* magazine and watching old episodes of *Perry Mason*. And you could still tell her anything. Those were the best times—snuggled up next to her, massaging her swollen feet, sleeping on the adjoining sofa so that if she needed to go to the bathroom in the middle of the night, she'd have help.

"And a one-ie and a two-ie and uuuup!" she'd say. Then, "Whoa," until the dizziness passed.

All this time, though she was planning her new house next door to us, she was getting very thin.

"I believe if I just had a milkshake," she'd drawl, "or a few shrimp .... " That was all we needed to hear, and we'd go tearing off to get whatever it was. It didn't matter when she ate only two bites of it.

One day, six-year-old Bekah came out in the yard where Kat was working and said, "Mama, Granny Jean wants some fresh pineapple." Kathleen said, "Pineapple! You tell Granny Jean to get up and go to Hawaii if she wants pineapple!" But we got it for her anyway.

After a while, she got too sick to be in the middle of things. I will never forget the sight of her frail body being lifted into the wheelchair, and her cries from the dizziness. She lay back in Kathleen's bedroom, looking up through the skylights at the branches over the roof. Jack and the girls moved in, and we were all with her when the pain came and the morphine eased it. There was a stillness around her more peaceful than if you'd been in there by yourself.

When I asked how she was, or if she wanted some glycerine to moisten her mouth, I felt as though I had interrupted a deeper conversation. One morning she woke up with her arms in the air saying, "Wonderful, wonderful! I have walked in sunny places in my dreams."

On the last night, I think we all knew what was happening, and we drew close.

"It won't be much longer now," Kathleen said. Granny Jean's breaths were shallow, and the veins in her neck barely pulsed. Kat crawled up in the bed, Laura and Beth lay on either side of her, and we took turns holding her hands. We dressed her in a pretty gown and sang to her.

Tell me why the stars do shine,
tell me why the ivy twines,
tell me why the sky's so blue
and I will tell you just why I love you.

Kathleen laid her hand on Granny Jean's chest and said, "Just one more breath now, sweetheart."

We were sprawled out on pillows, on the bed, in chairs, on the floor, just like at her slumber parties. Except this time, we'd wake up in different places. We'd be right where we laid our heads the night before. And Granny Jean would be walking in sunny places, waving her arms and saying, "Wonderful, wonderful!"

Rebecca Stanborough spent her teenage years in a ramshackle community house with twenty-one people and two bathrooms. Now she lives and writes in St. Augustine, Florida, surrounded by alligators, island rats, and roseate spoonbills, none of whom has ever asked to share her bathroom.

ALL TREASURES

BY PATTI KIM

When asked what I ate for dinner, I lied. It was roasted chicken, mashed potatoes, and salad, rather than the kimchi, rice, and fermented bean soup drowning beheaded anchovies.

When asked what my parents did for a living, I lied. To say they were orthodontists, lawyers, plastic surgeons, or president of Woodward and Lothrop was too far-fetched. So I told them they owned a restaurant called The Greenhouse in Silver Spring on Georgia Avenue. The seafood was especially good there. Fresh. When really, my mom and dad worked in a carryout in Southeast D.C. Mom made hog maw, ham hocks, fat back, chitlins, and chicken gizzards in gravy. Dad worked the register, taking money and making change. They served poor-people food to the poor.

When asked who did my hair and where I got it done, I lied. It was Sabine at Harlowe Salon in Georgetown, rather than my mom, dad, or sister in our basement with the company of a circular saw, an electric drill, hammers, screws, and wood scraps. Our hidden do-it-yourself den.

When asked where I got my cute skirt, I lied. Hecht's, Woodies, or Saks. When really it was something I stitched together from scraps of fabric left over from my mom's annual sewing of aprons for work.

Moving from Riverdale, a neighborhood of low-income families and mostly immigrants, to Potomac, the birthplace of Darren Star—future creator of *Beverly Hills 90210*, *Melrose Place* and *Sex and the City*—jarred me. (By the way, Darren and I went to the same high school, which inspired *90210*.) My teen logic said that for me to survive my new environment, I must lie, pretend, and fictionalize. My reality was a shame. It must not be found out. I must not be found.

I got good at lying. I got hooked on it. Pulling one over on a poor soul gave me a high. Catching the brief flicker of envy in eyes gratified. It was about time the others turned green.

I got through high school, protected myself from any imagined humiliation, and avoided genuine friendships. It was lonely, but I successfully kept secret the reality of my life at home, which was built on the hard work of my parents, homemade skirts, free haircuts, and kimchi. All hidden. All treasures.

Patti Kim was born in Busan, Korea. Raised in Maryland on both sides of the tracks. Author of A Cab Called Reliable *and* Here I Am. *Married with kids, but can't stop writing about her childhood.*

LETTER TO MY SIXTEEN-YEAR-OLD SELF

BY ALISON MCGHEE

Dear Sixteen-Year-Old Self,

This is the only photo of you I could find. You held an Instamatic out in front of you, hoping somehow to capture your own face, and pressed the little black button. I remember exactly when you took that photo. You had just gotten out of the shower. You were wearing cut-offs and that blue work shirt you wore every day back then.

You wondered if maybe you could capture something in a photo that would tell you something you didn't know about yourself.

Now I look at that photo and I think: You were on the verge. Of so much.

You don't think of yourself as unhappy right now. You go to high school out in the country, you have friends, you belong to a bunch of things. You don't think of yourself as lonely.

But in retrospect, you're waiting and you don't even know it. You're waiting for the doors of your life to blow open, for the sky to lift high overhead.

What can I tell you now, from this long perspective of time?

You can let up some. You think you have to push yourself every day, that you have to maintain some high, rigid standard, be ultra-disciplined, but you don't. Why are you setting your alarm every morning for 4:45? So sleepy.

Then again, that discipline will come in handy years later, when you have three little kids—yes! you do end up with three kids, just like you wanted!—and you get up at four because it's the only time you can write in silence.

So many things that you think matter so much right now do not, in the end, matter. Or they matter, but in a way that you're too young to understand yet.

That one night you're thinking about, when they took off and left you there? When you get to my age, instead of blaming yourself—too ugly, too boring, all my fault—you'll shrug and think, it's clear that whatever I was back then, I at least wasn't mean.

All those times on the school bus, in school, walking the dirt roads past broken-down trailers, when you feel helpless in the face of others' pain, will eventually be transformed into art. Even if you feel right now as if you'll break apart from it, it will be worth it.

Most everything that you are going to live through will, in the end, be worth it.

It's too late to go back and re-do things, but if I could, I'd tell you a few things that you're too young to know:

When your grandmother and your father and your mother tell you not to change your plans, that the tickets are nonrefundable, that he knew how much you loved him, don't listen to them. Go to your grandfather's funeral, because when you don't, you will forever regret it.

You don't need to wash your hair every day.

Don't listen when people tell you that love fades, that it becomes humdrum, ordinary, that this is the way it is for everyone. It's not.

You are not ugly the way you fear you are.

Don't be so afraid, out of self-consciousness, of trying things that it seems as if everyone around you already knows how to do. Skiing, for example. In two years you're going to go to a college that has its own snow bowl; learn to ski.

Four years from now, when that boy you have the massive crush on comes to your room in Hepburn Hall with a bottle of wine and a bunch of roses, invite him in. Do not stand there in dumb shyness, your heart beating like a hummingbird, and thank him politely and watch his face fall and say good night and shut the door. Because that's something else you're going to regret forever.

When you're afraid of something, tell someone.

When you need help, ask for it.

When your insides are whirling around and you feel as if

you're drowning, panicking and desperate, don't put a calm smile on your face and walk around as if you're fine.

There are lots of people who would love to help you.

There are lots of people who love you. You don't know that yet, but you will.

In some ways, you're going to live your life in reverse of most people your age. Awful things are going to happen to you when you're young, and you're going to feel much older than your friends. For many years your interior will not match your exterior.

But guess what? Time will go by, and your friends will catch up to you. Life catches up to everyone. The older you get the happier you get, the more rebellious, the less willing to suffer fools, to put up with bad behavior. You're going to feel so free when you get older.

You are going to be so much happier when you're older than you can believe possible right now. Most of that happiness will come when you let go of trying to come across a certain way, when you just let people see you for who you are.

It makes me sad that this is going to take you a long time to learn, and I wish I could change it for you, but I can't.

So many years from the day you held that camera out and hoped this photo would reveal something you couldn't explain, something you wanted so badly to know about yourself, you will look at it and feel this big sweep of love for that young girl, her whole life stretching out before her, as if she isn't you.

But she is.

Alison McGhee writes in all forms for all ages. She's the #1 New York Times *bestselling author of books such as* Shadow Baby *and* Someday *and a slew of others. She lives in Minneapolis and Vermont, is irresistibly drawn to the color green, and would be happy to eat potstickers every day.*

INDEX BY SUBJECT

AUTHOR INDEX